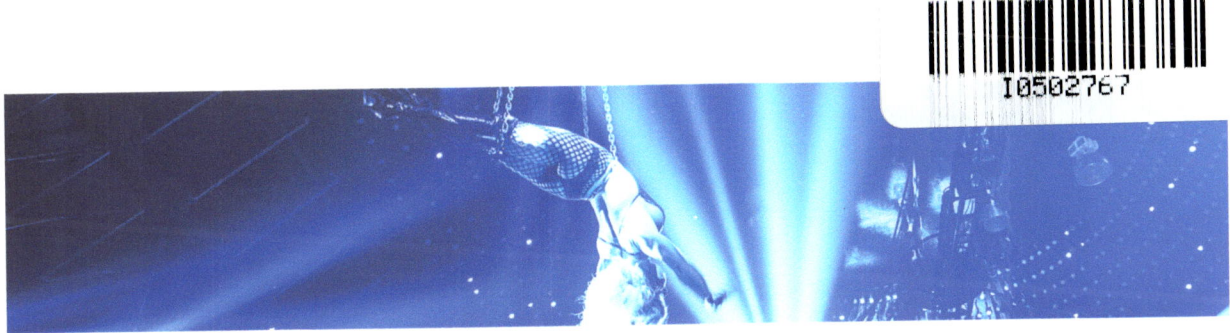

ARTISTE STATMENT

Welcome to NIGHTLIFE where only glimmers of light exist and movements become sexy silhouettes of reality meeting your fantasies. In a world filled with beautiful occurrences, I developed this series of photographs to capture what some may consider a strange world. However, it is the beauty in the performances and the movements of the performers in low light who tantalize the audience to create art.

Here is your V.I.P band to enter into that world of celebration and NIGHTLIFE as it exists today.

BY

Rodney Stewart

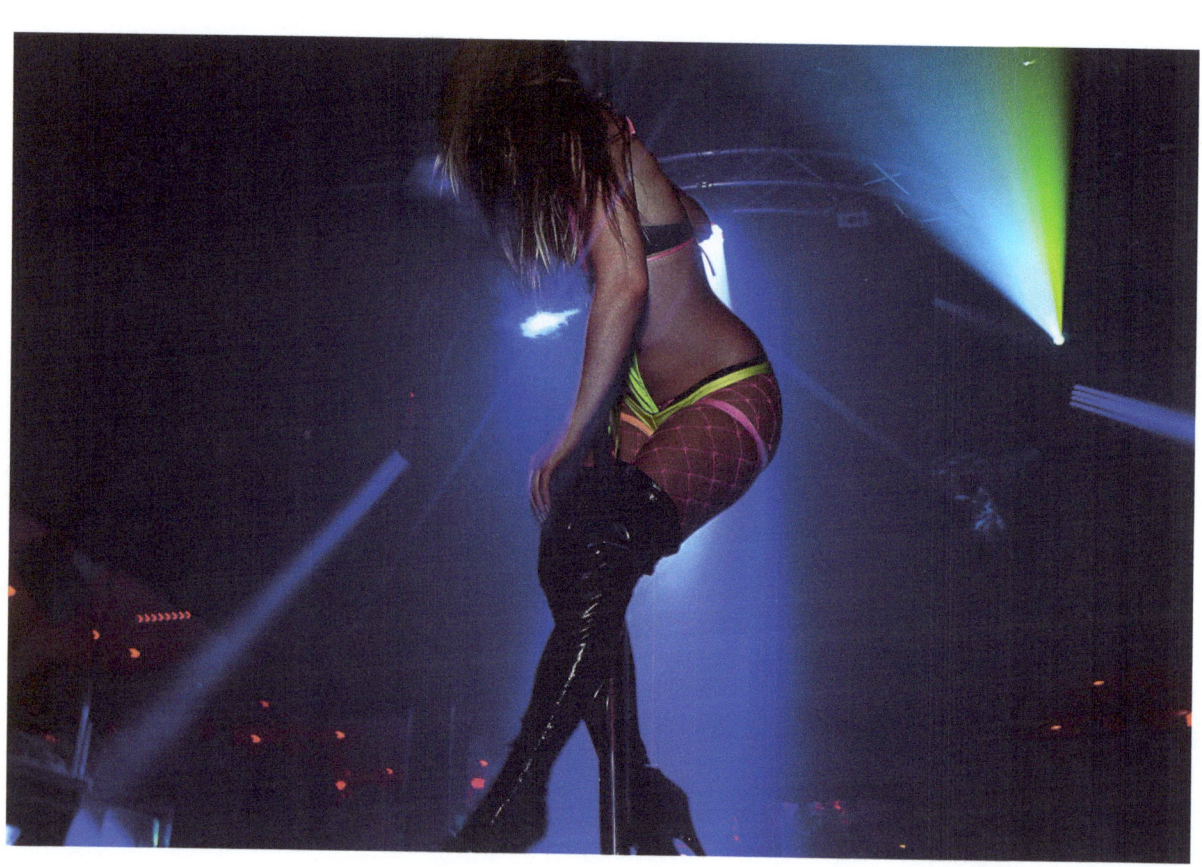

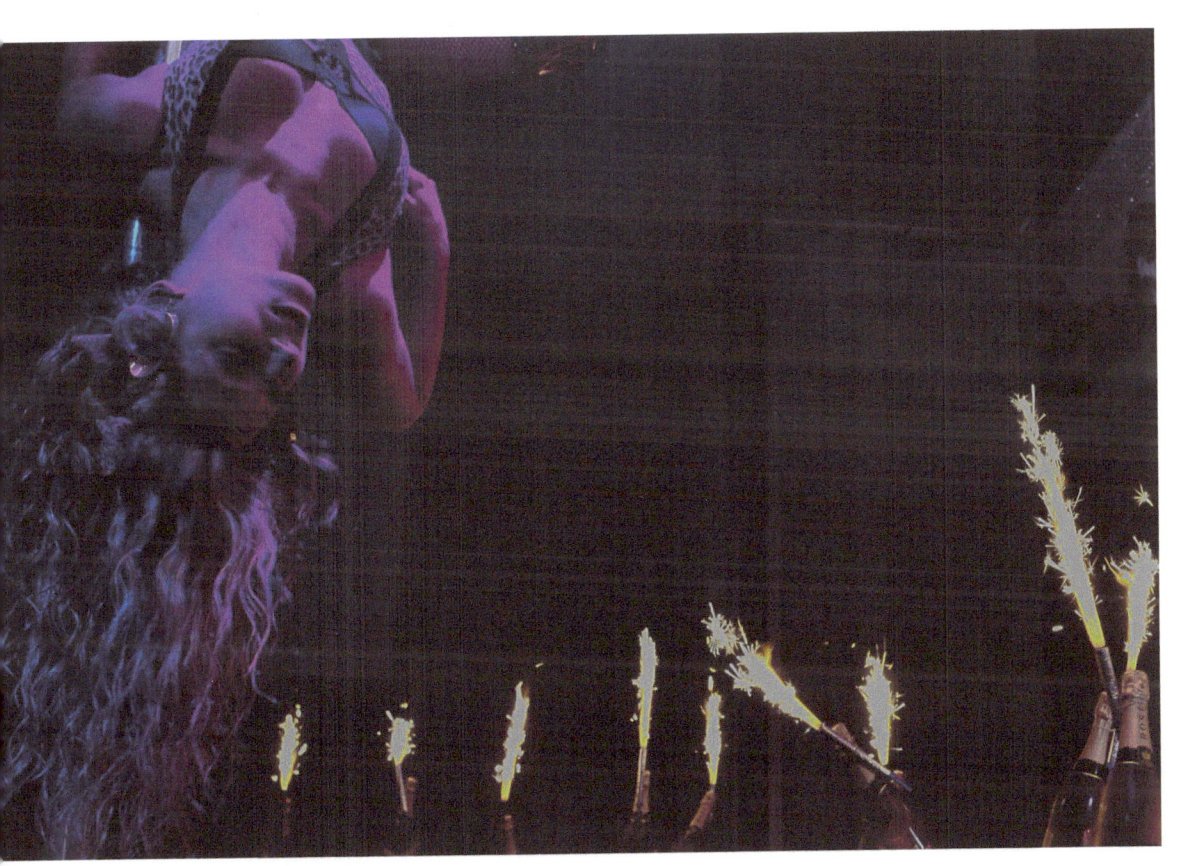

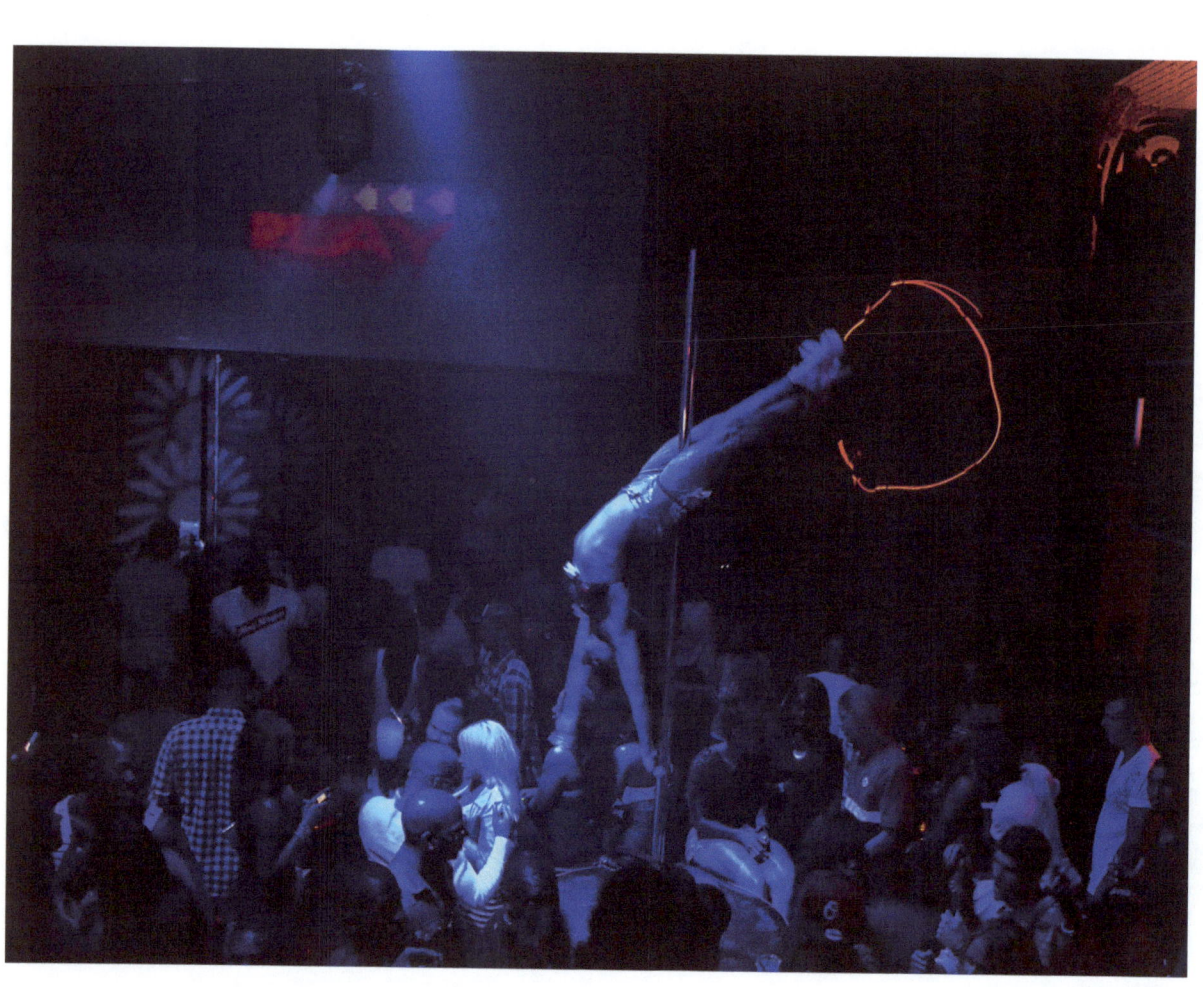

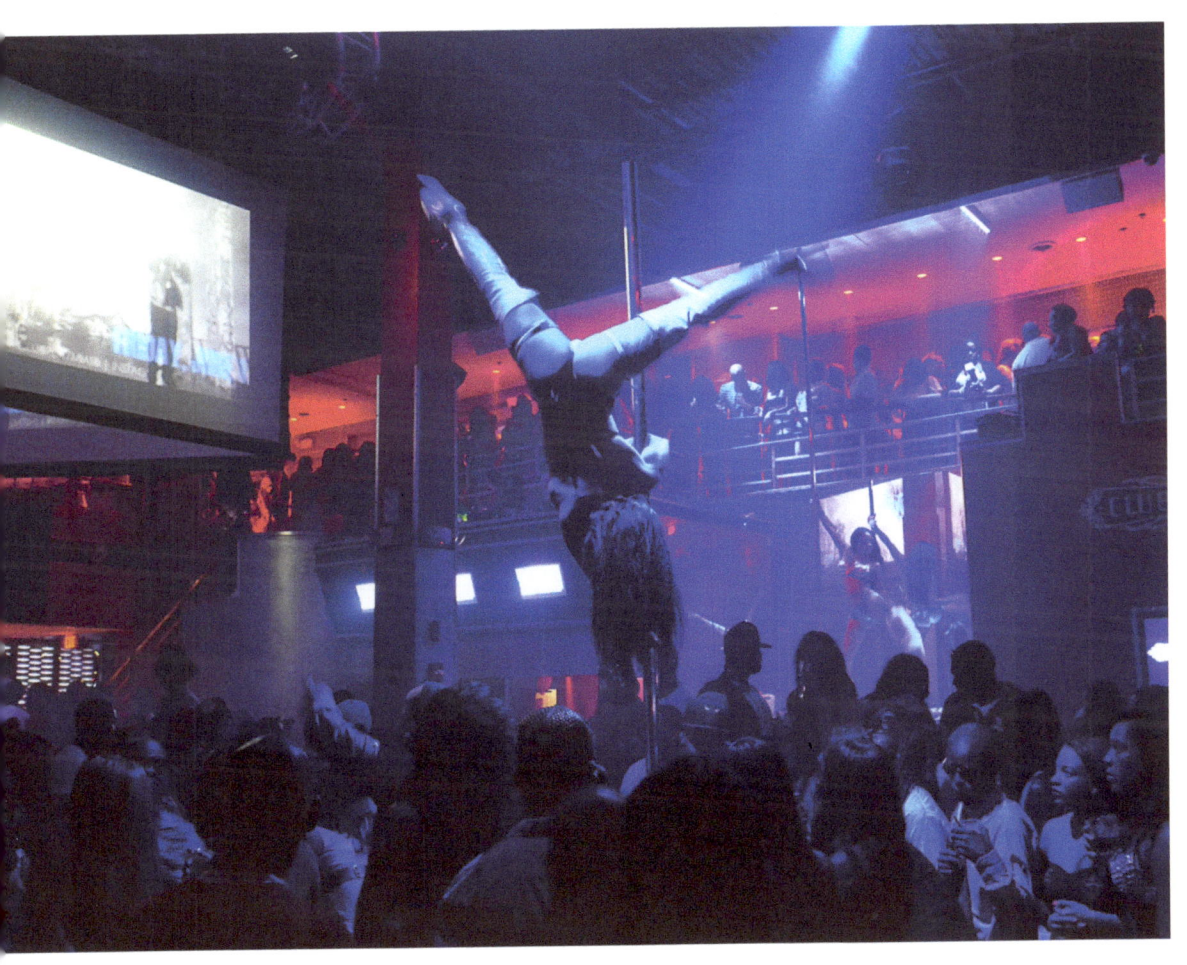

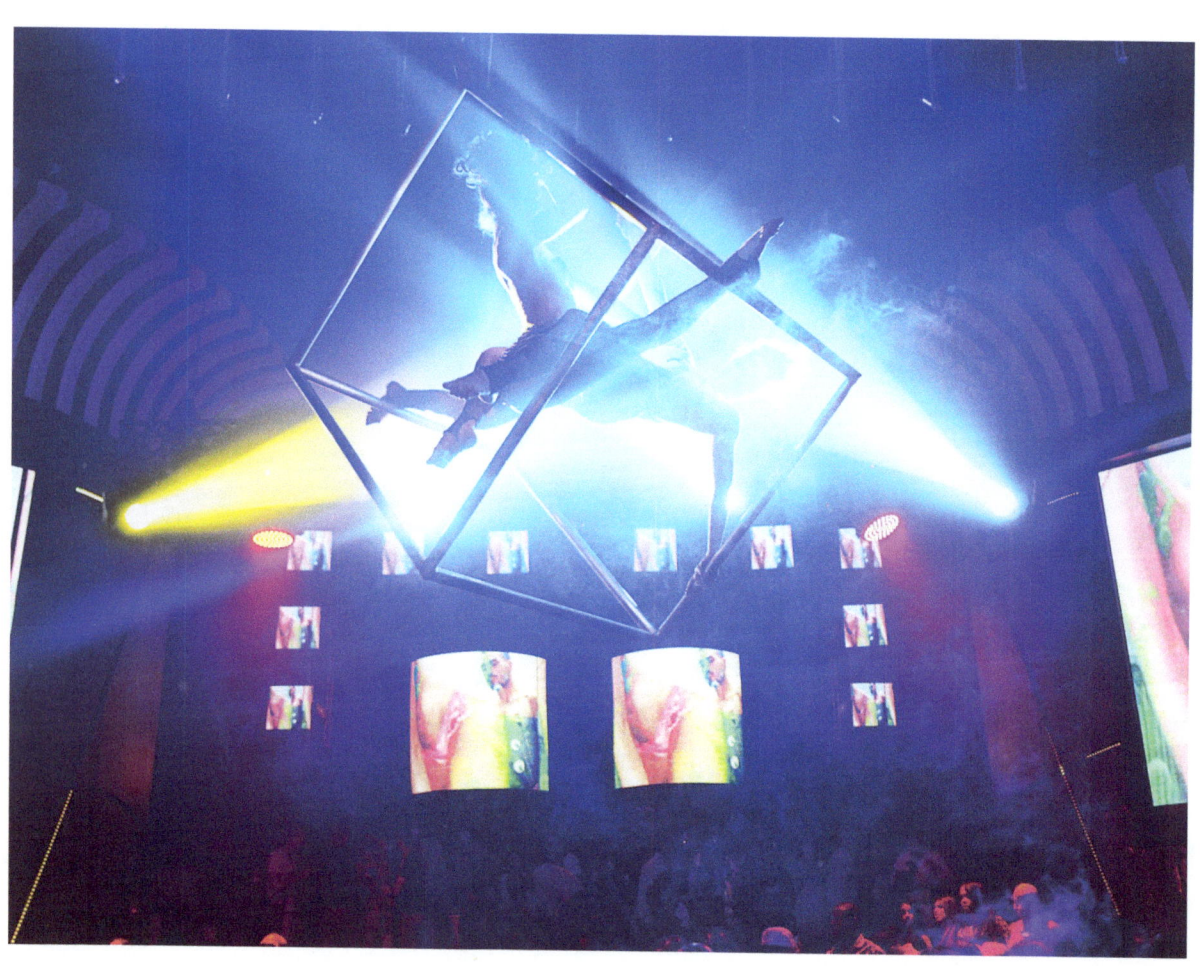

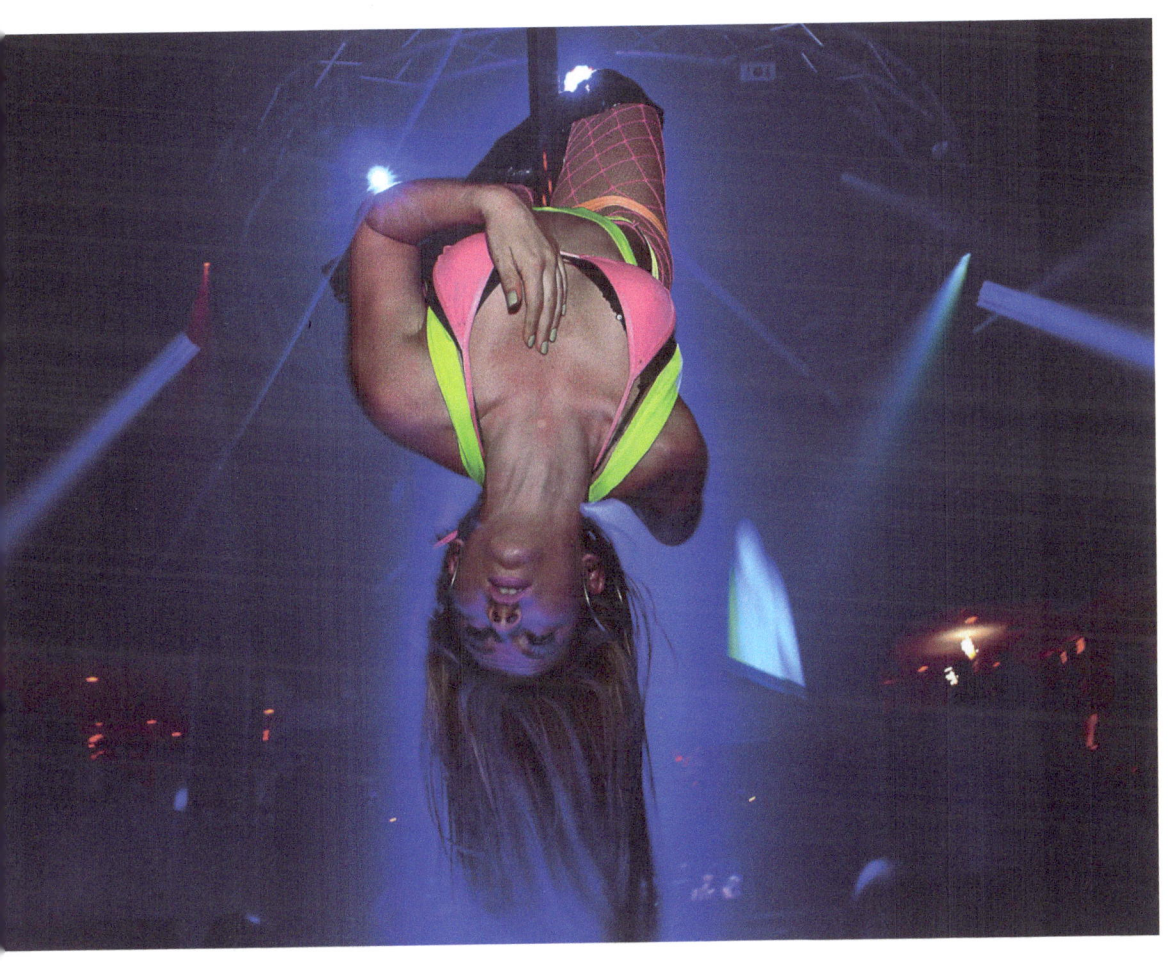

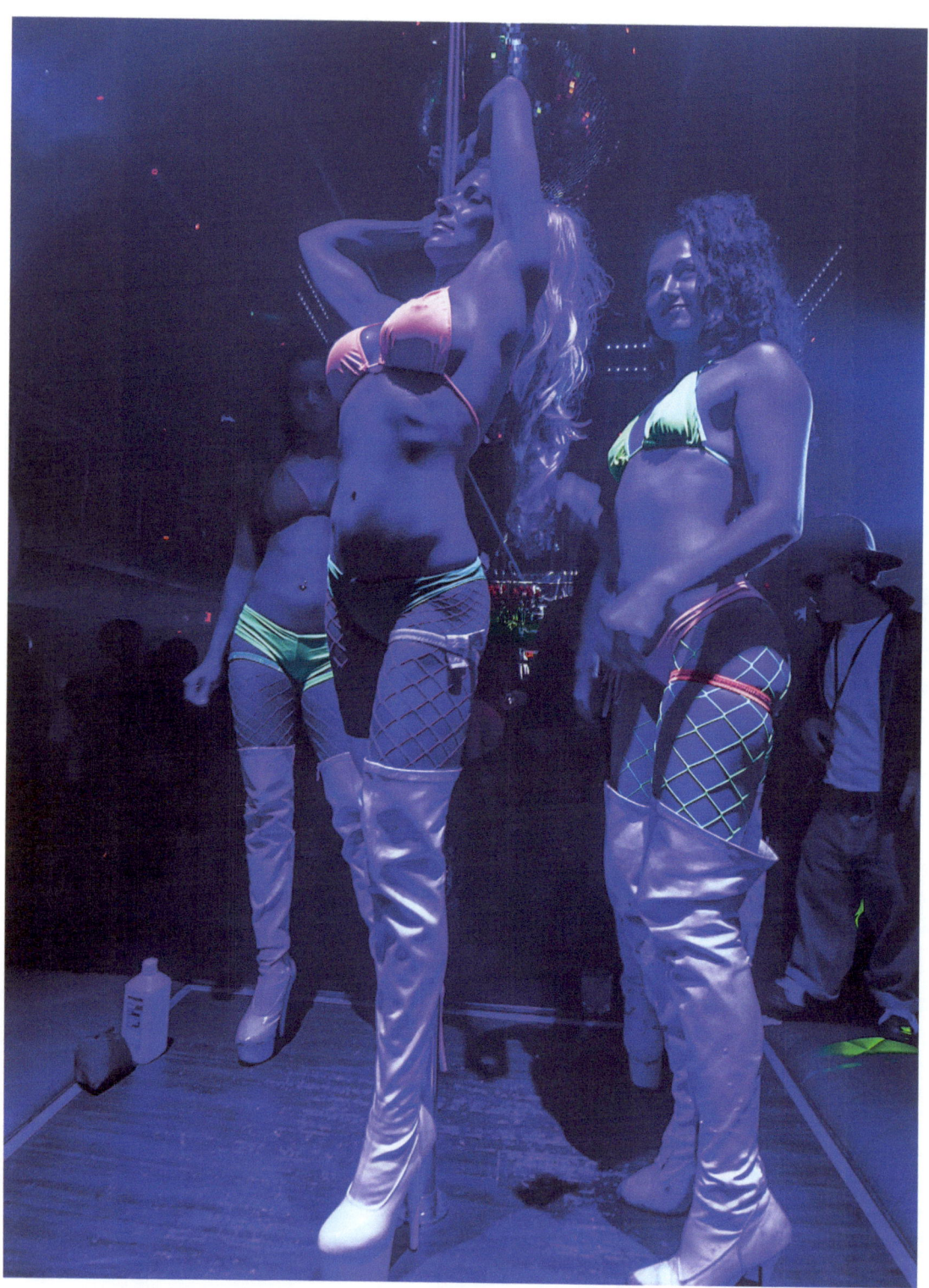

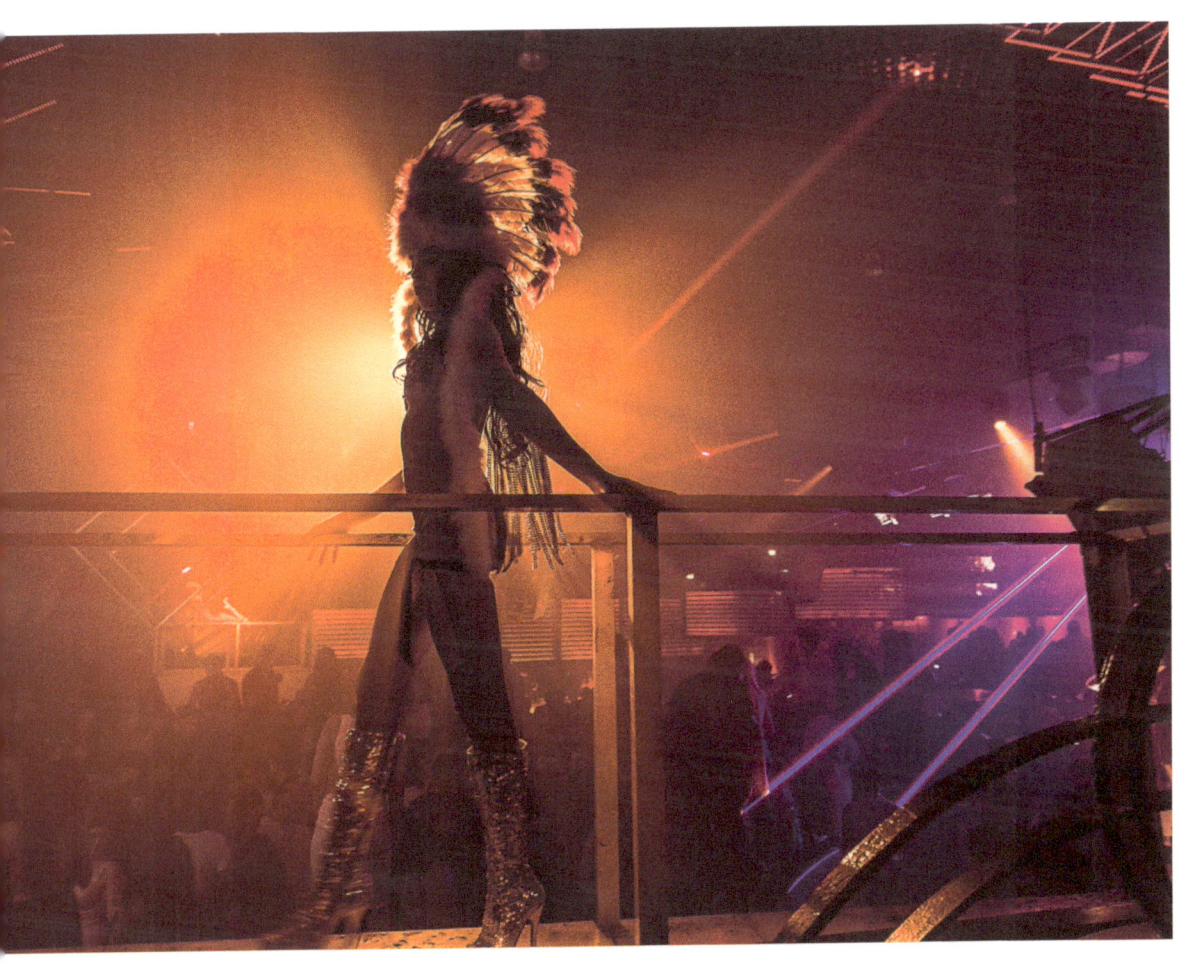

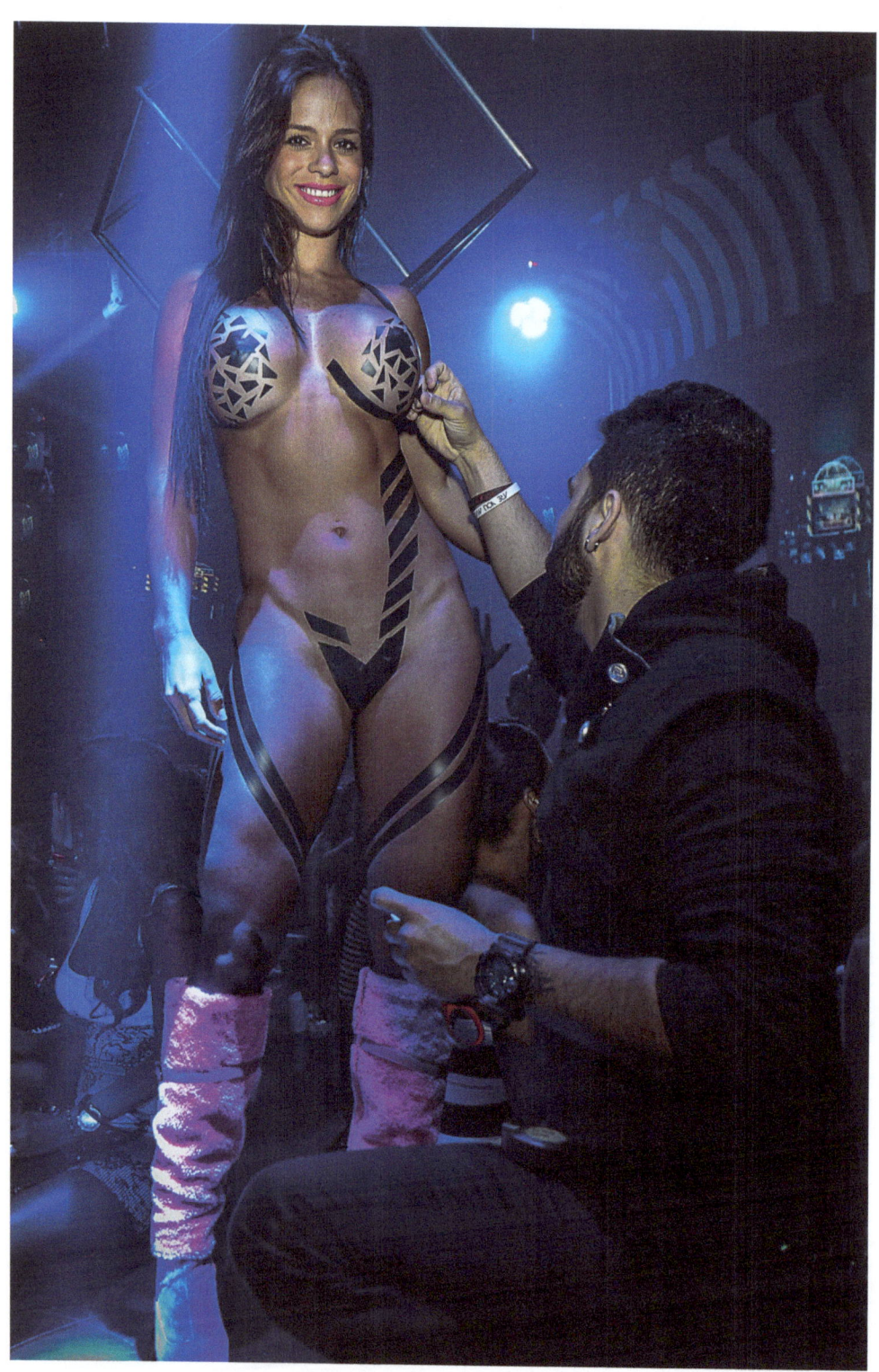

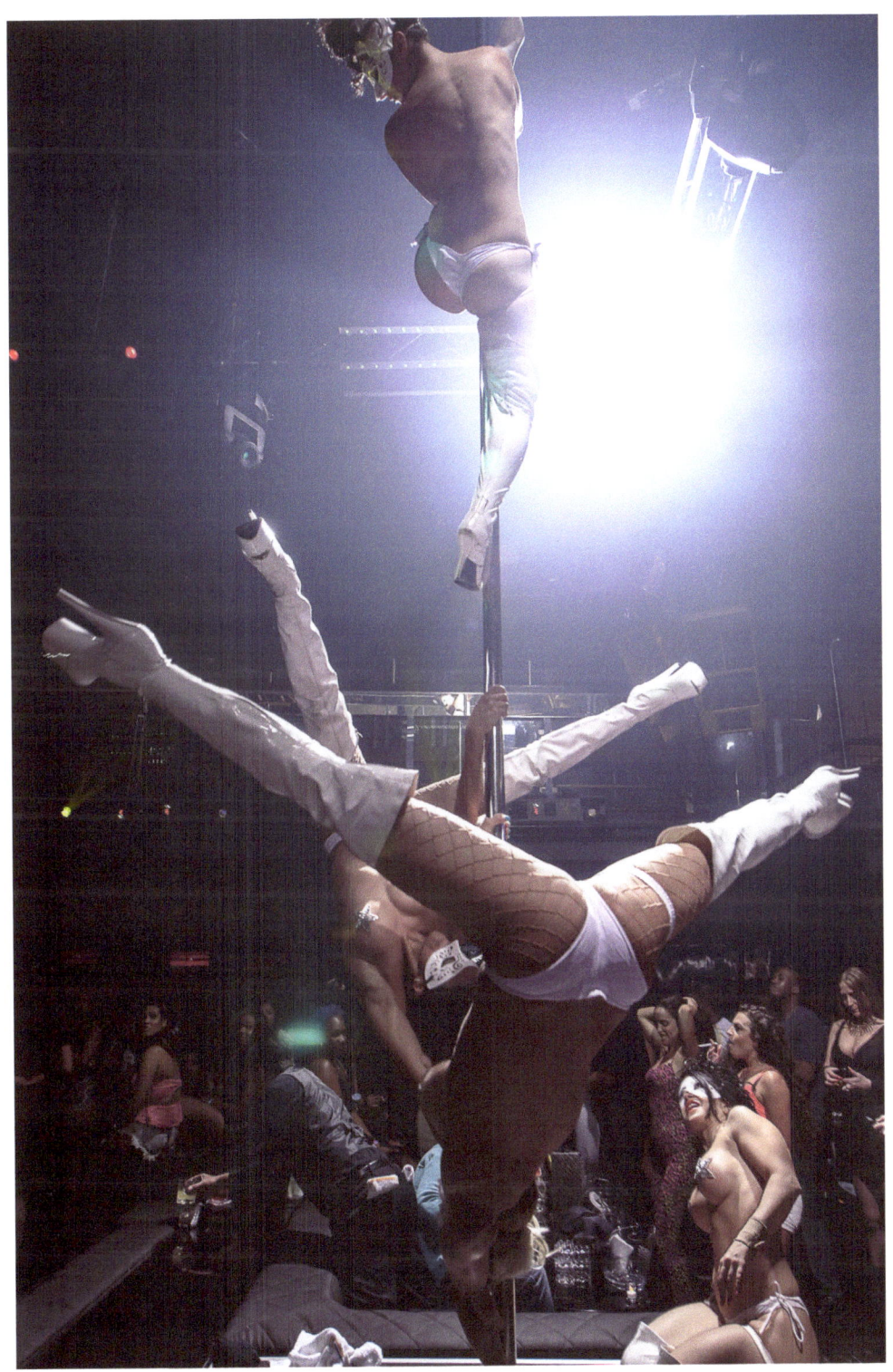

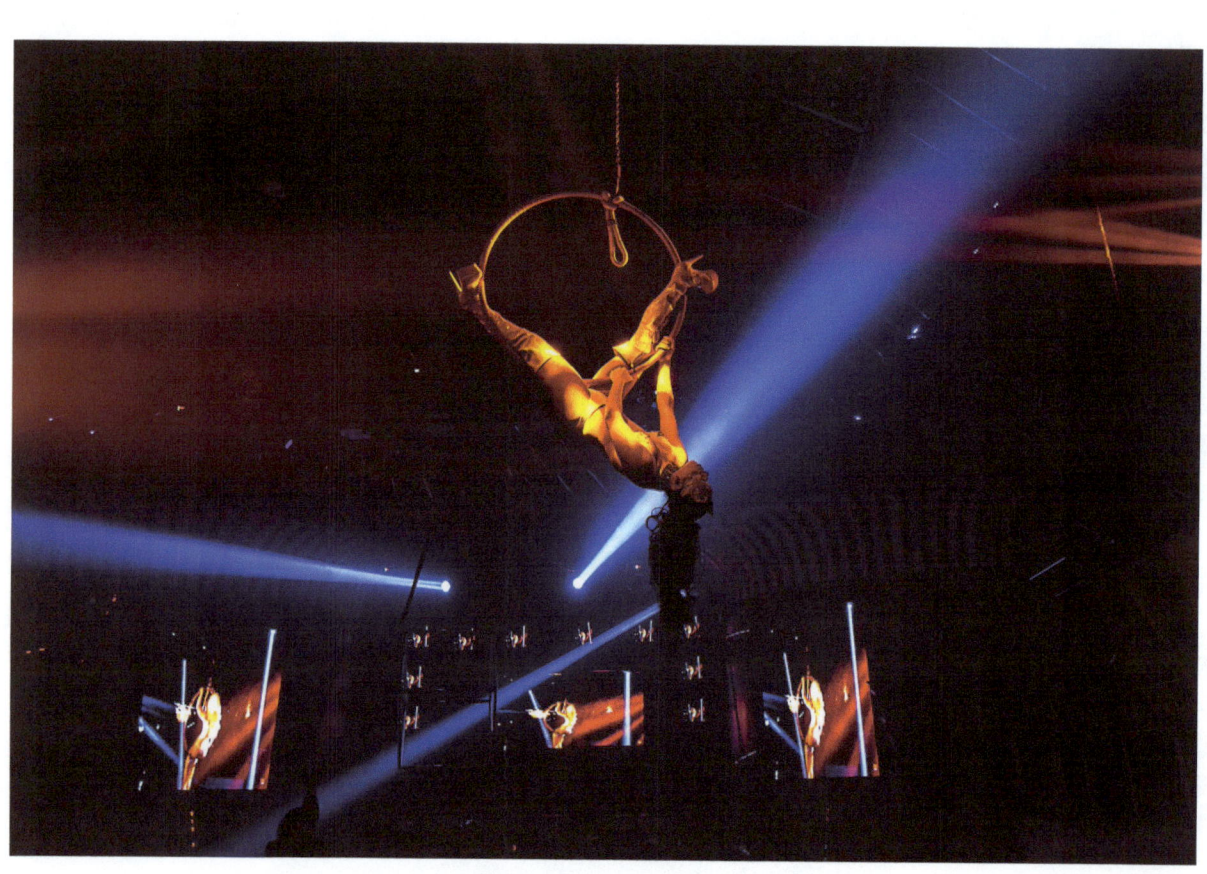

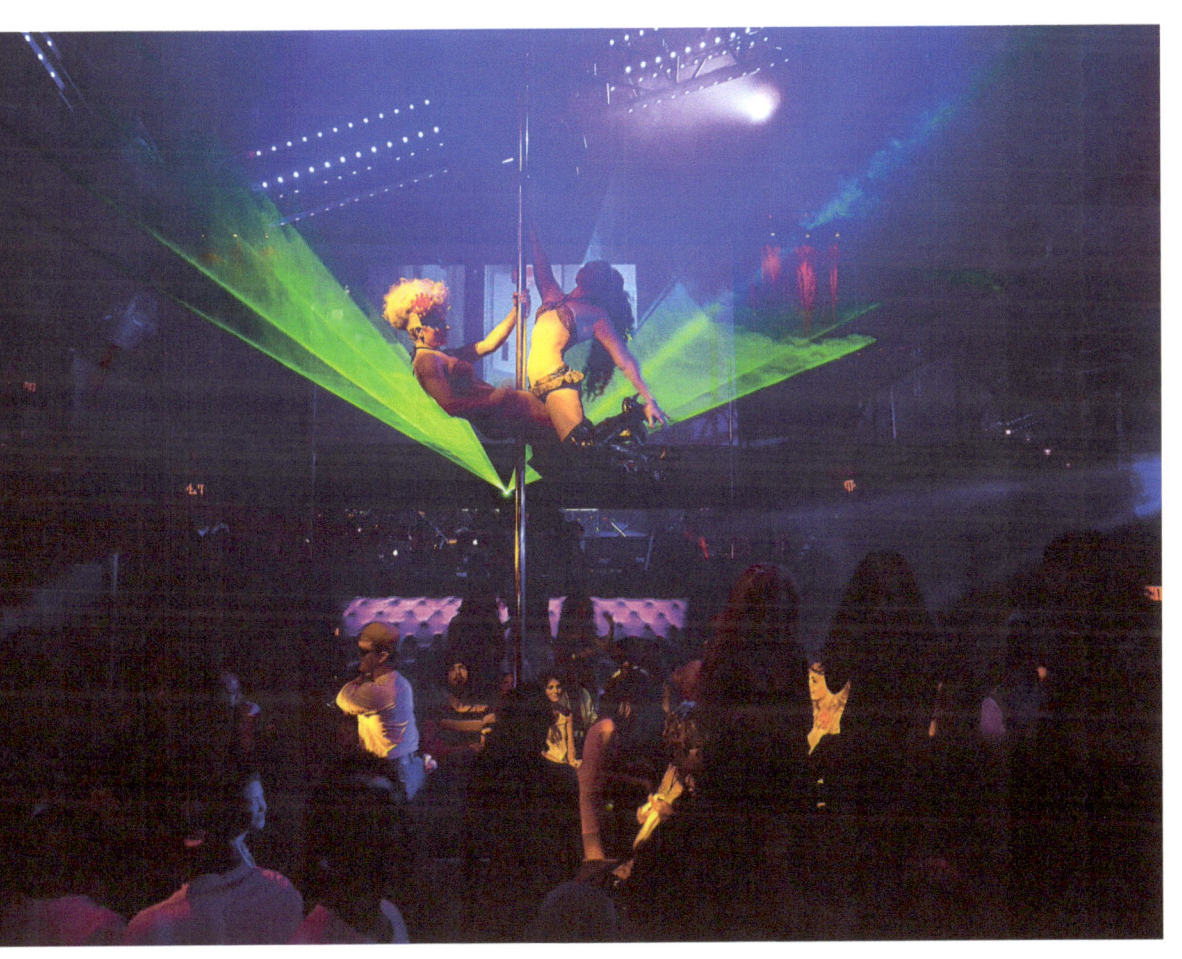

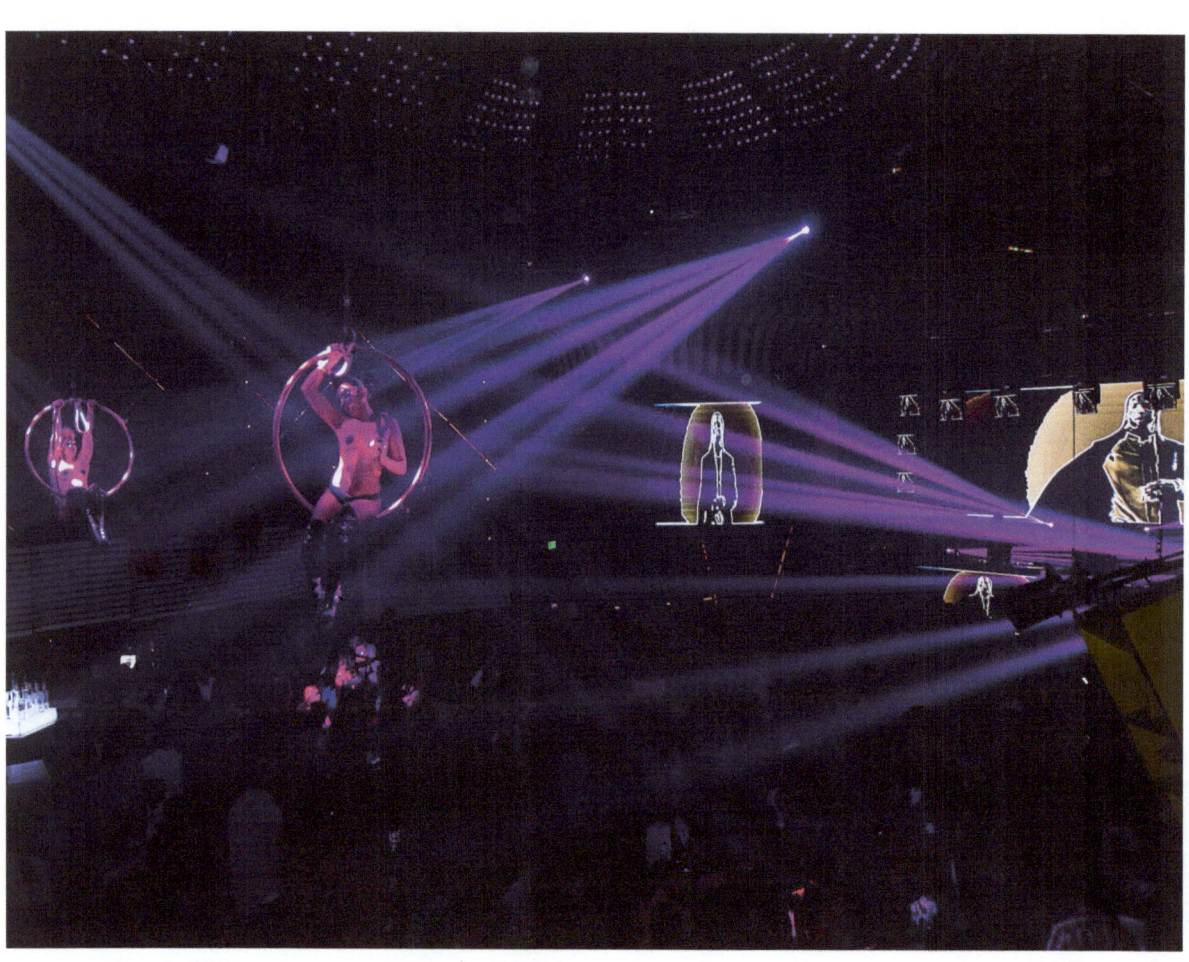

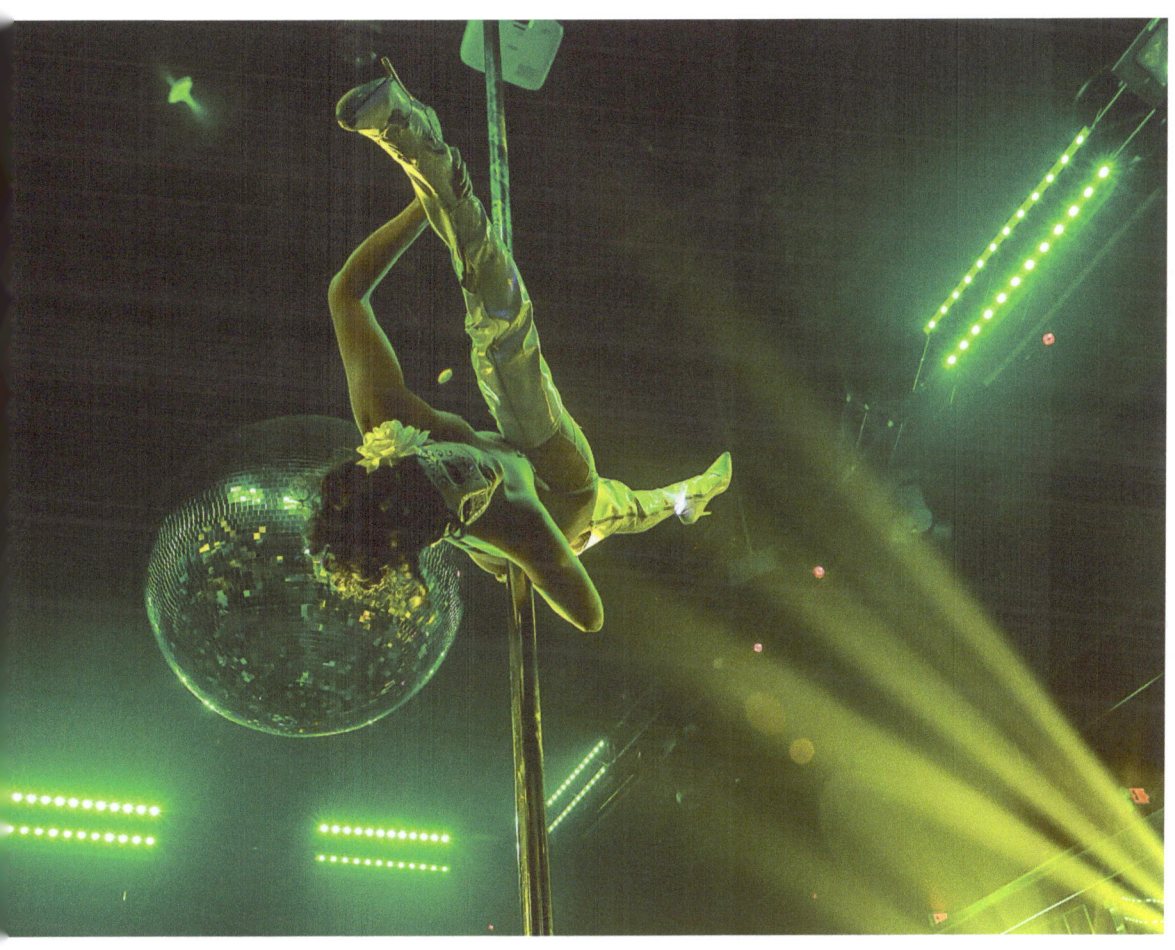

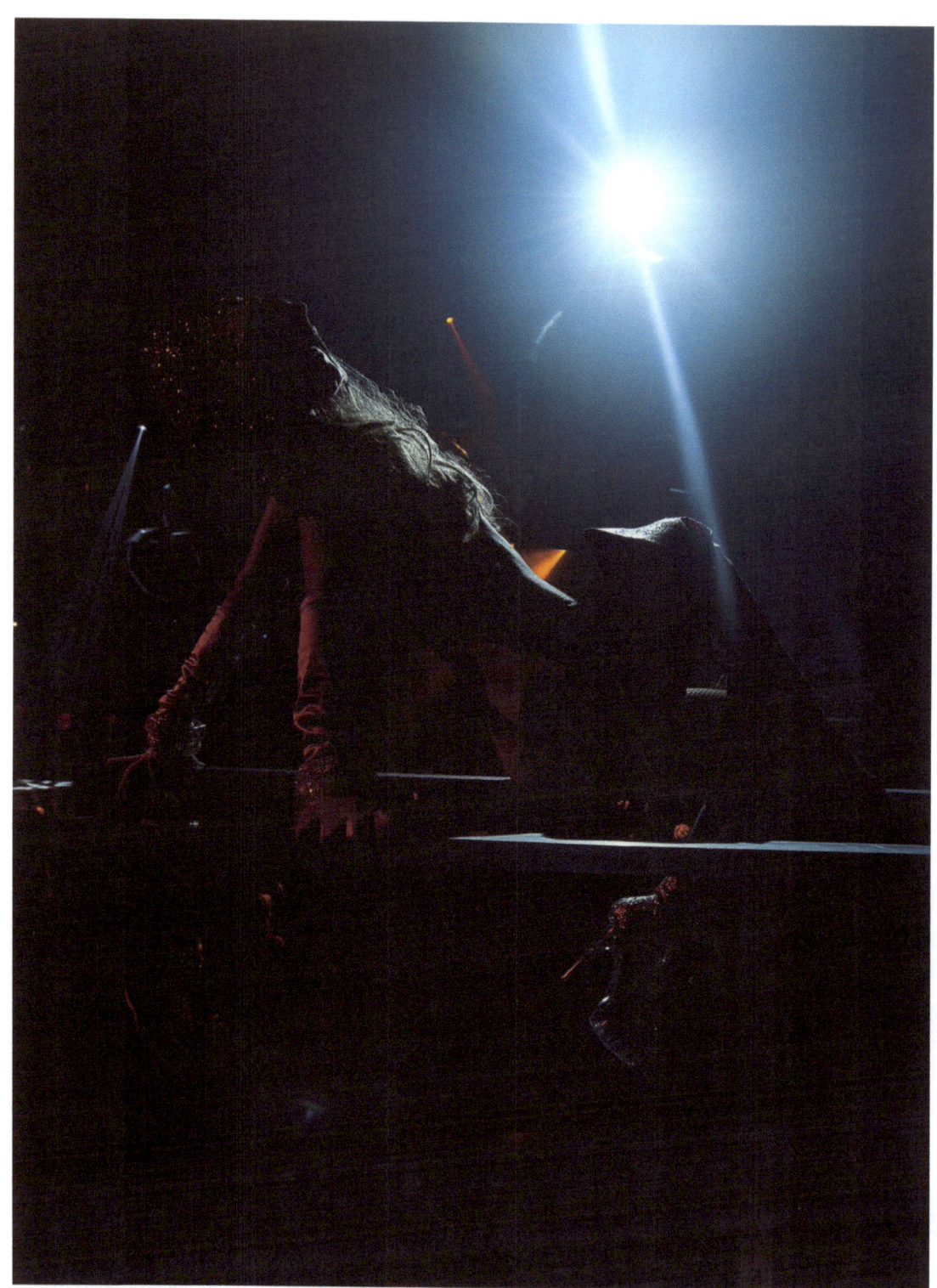

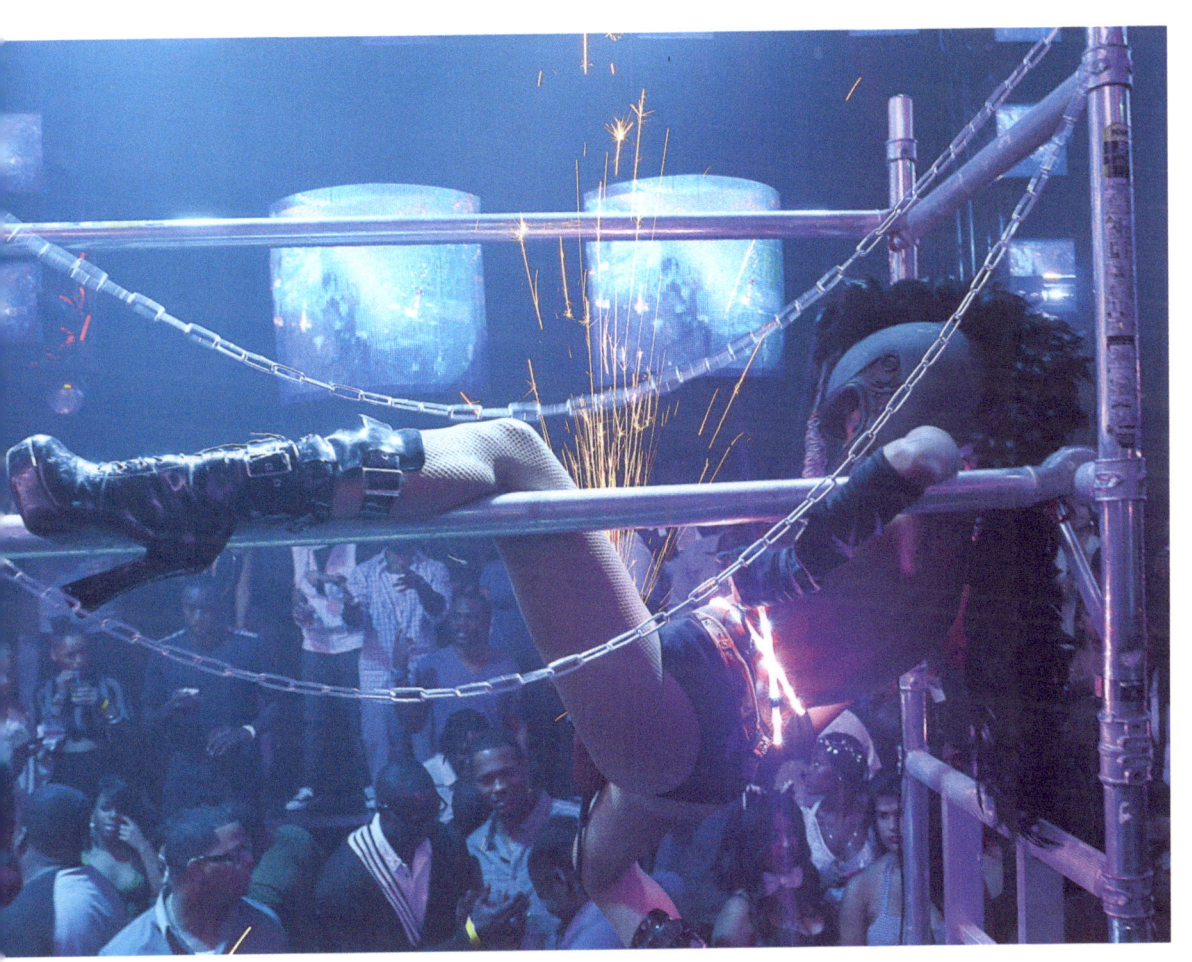

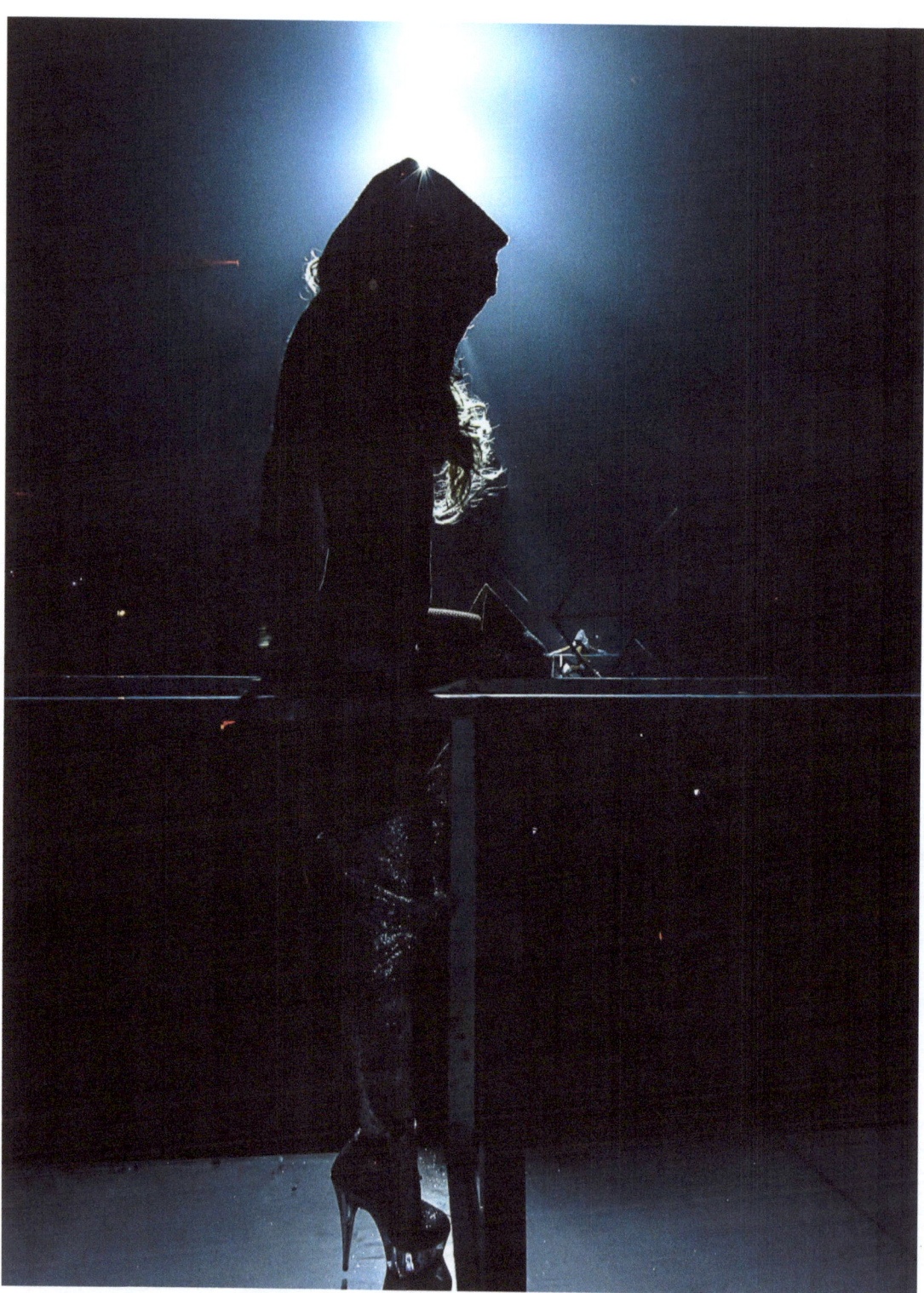

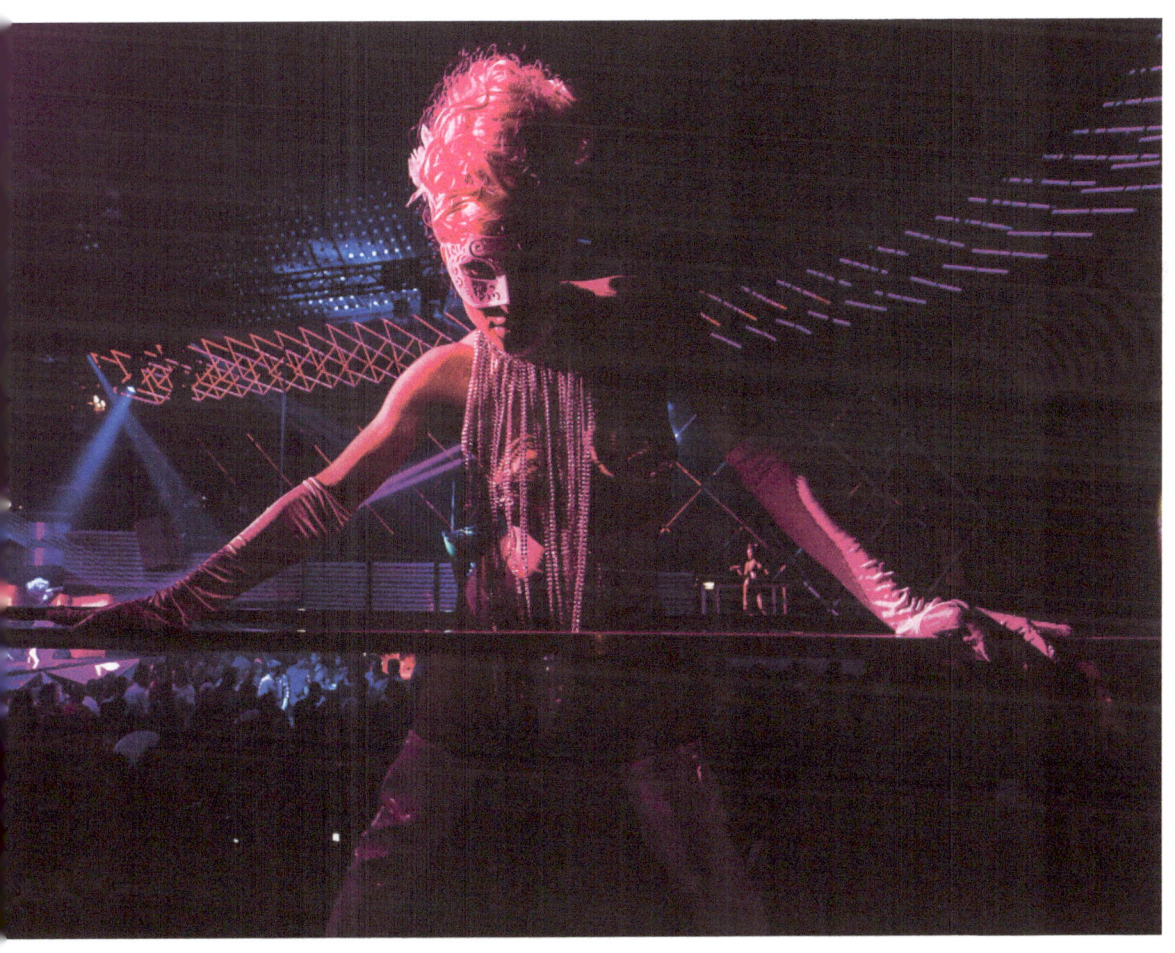

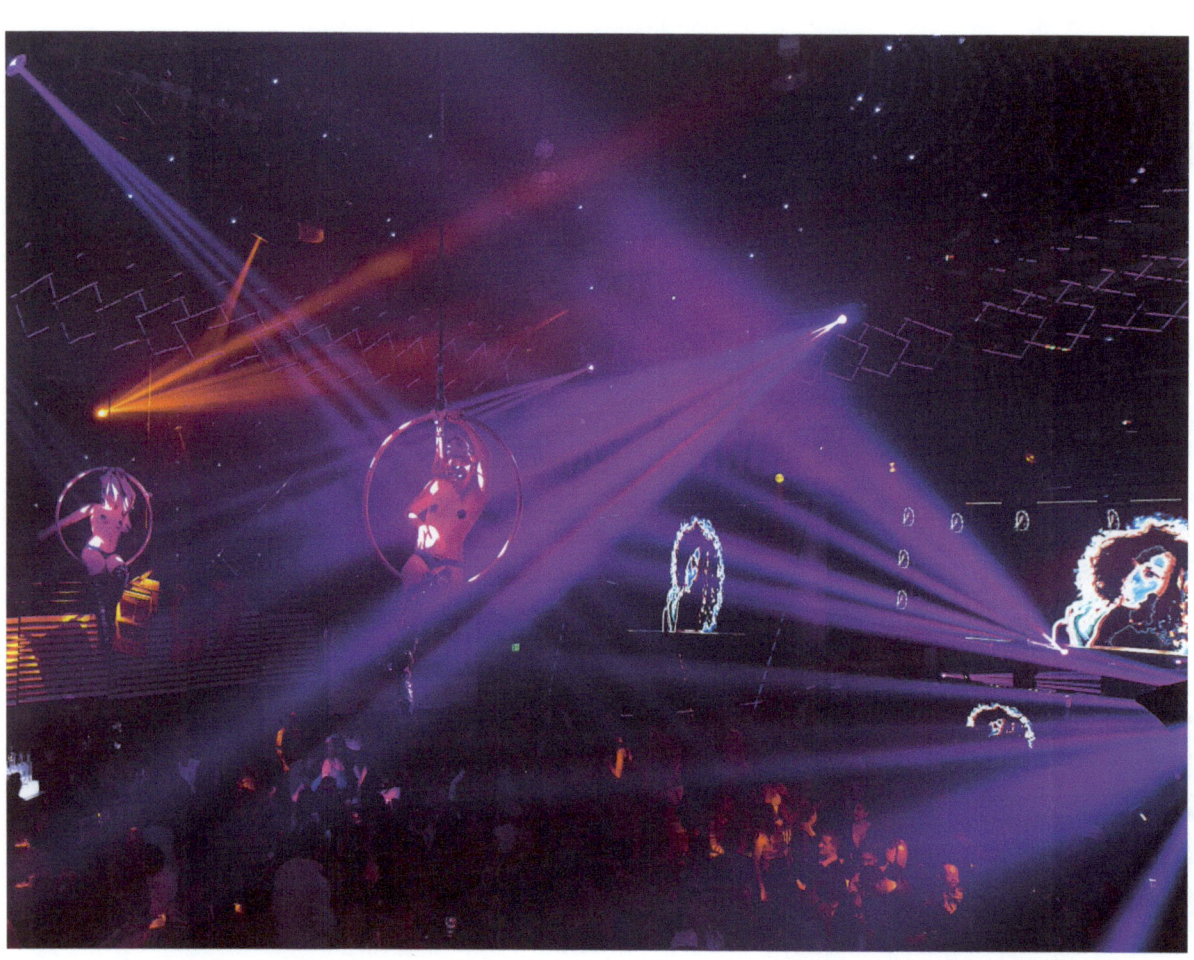

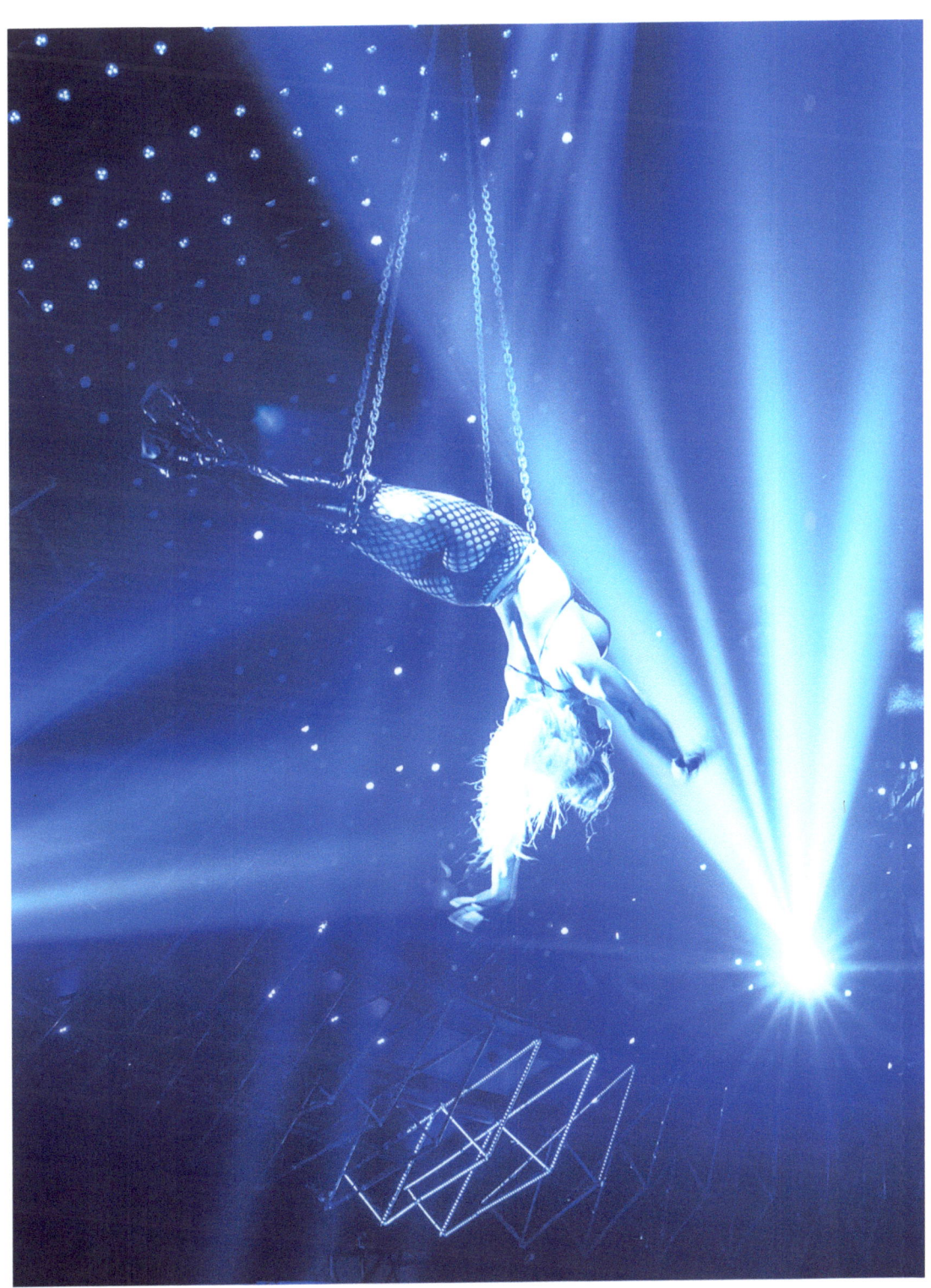

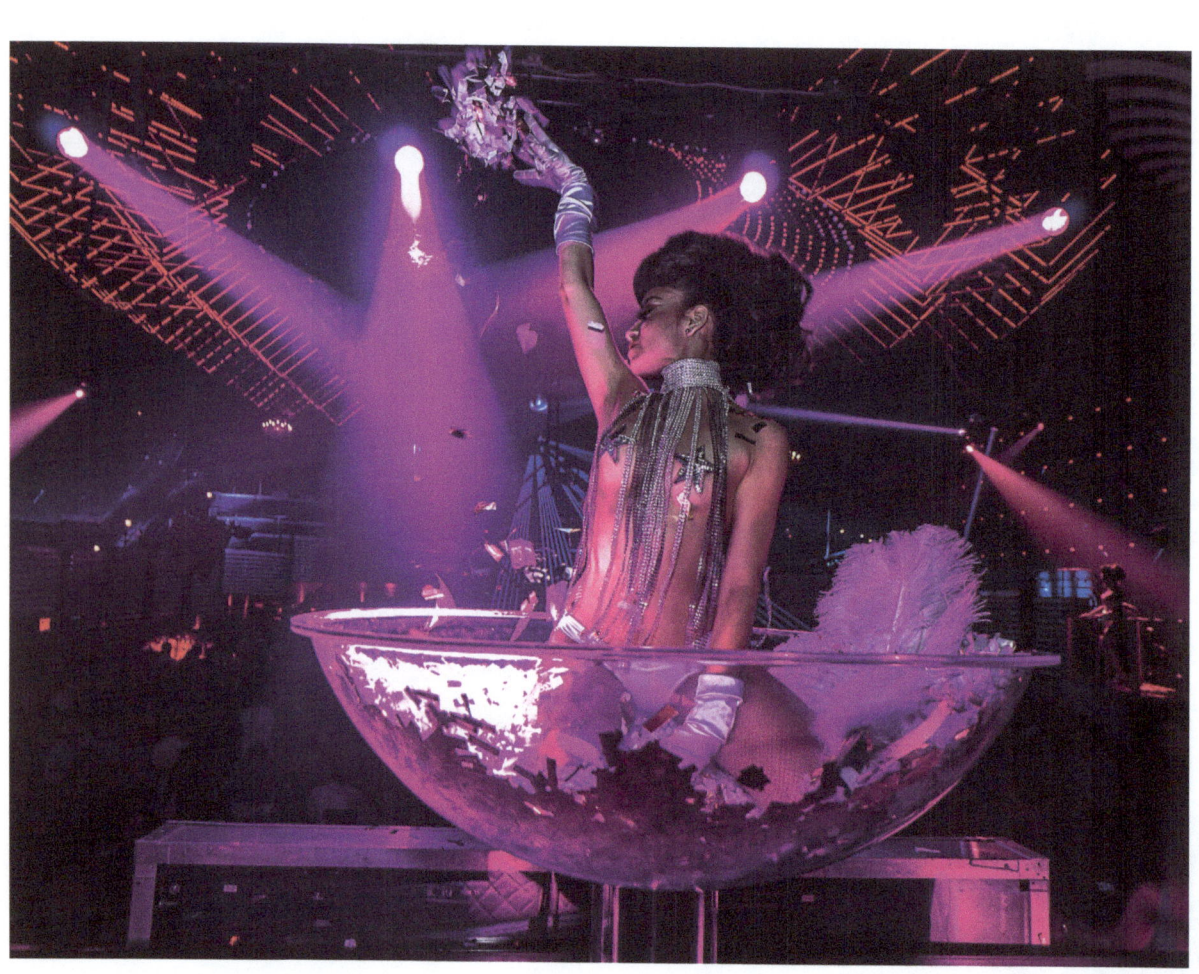

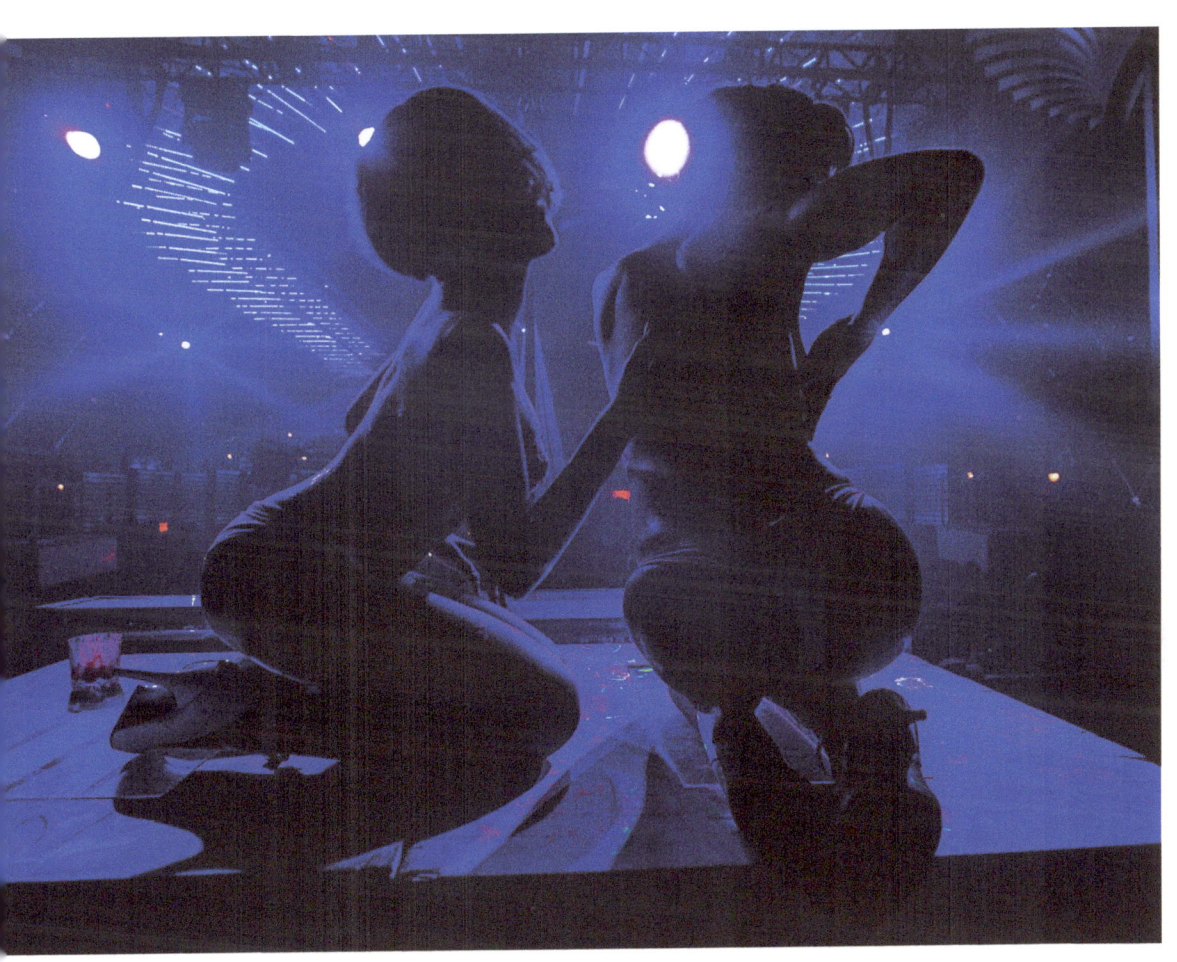

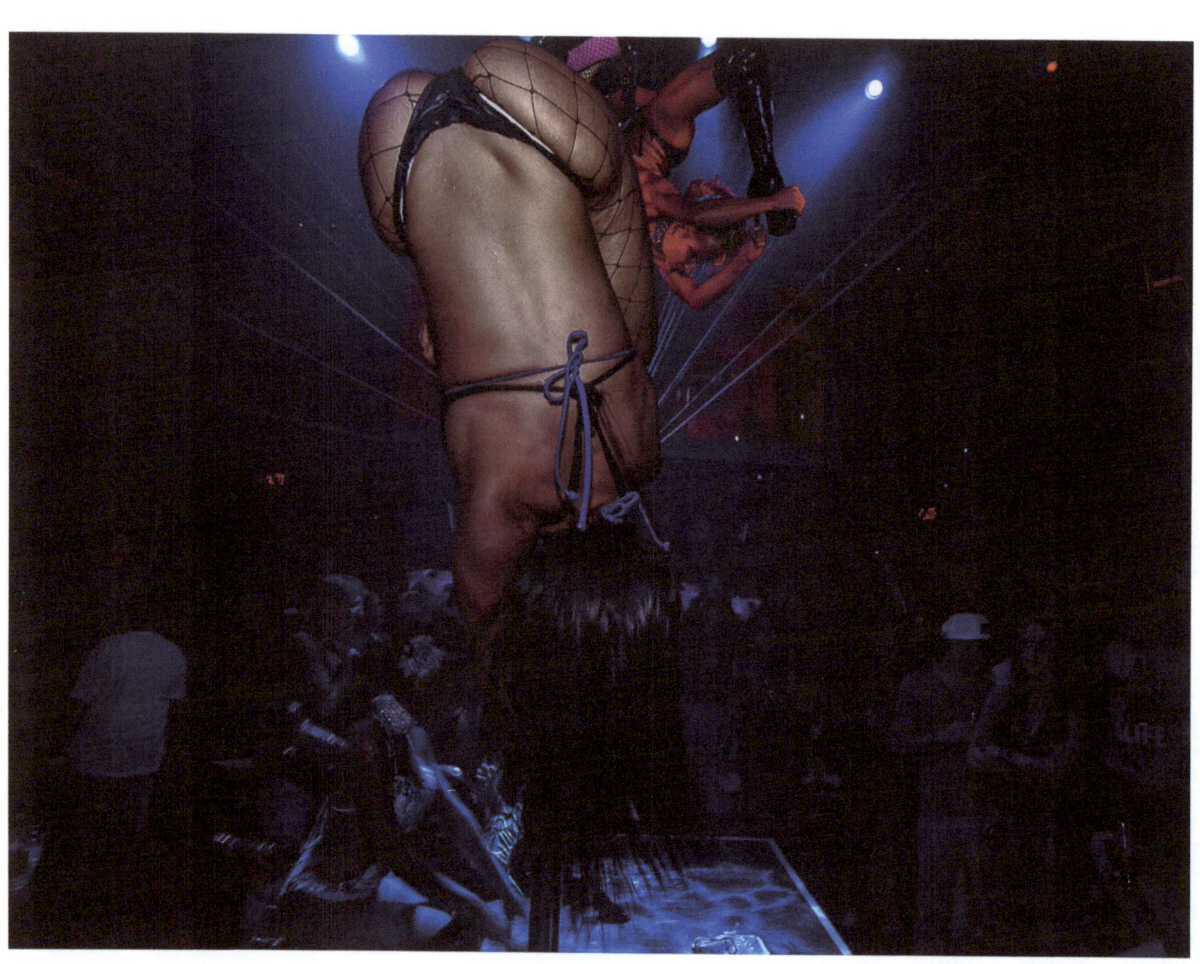

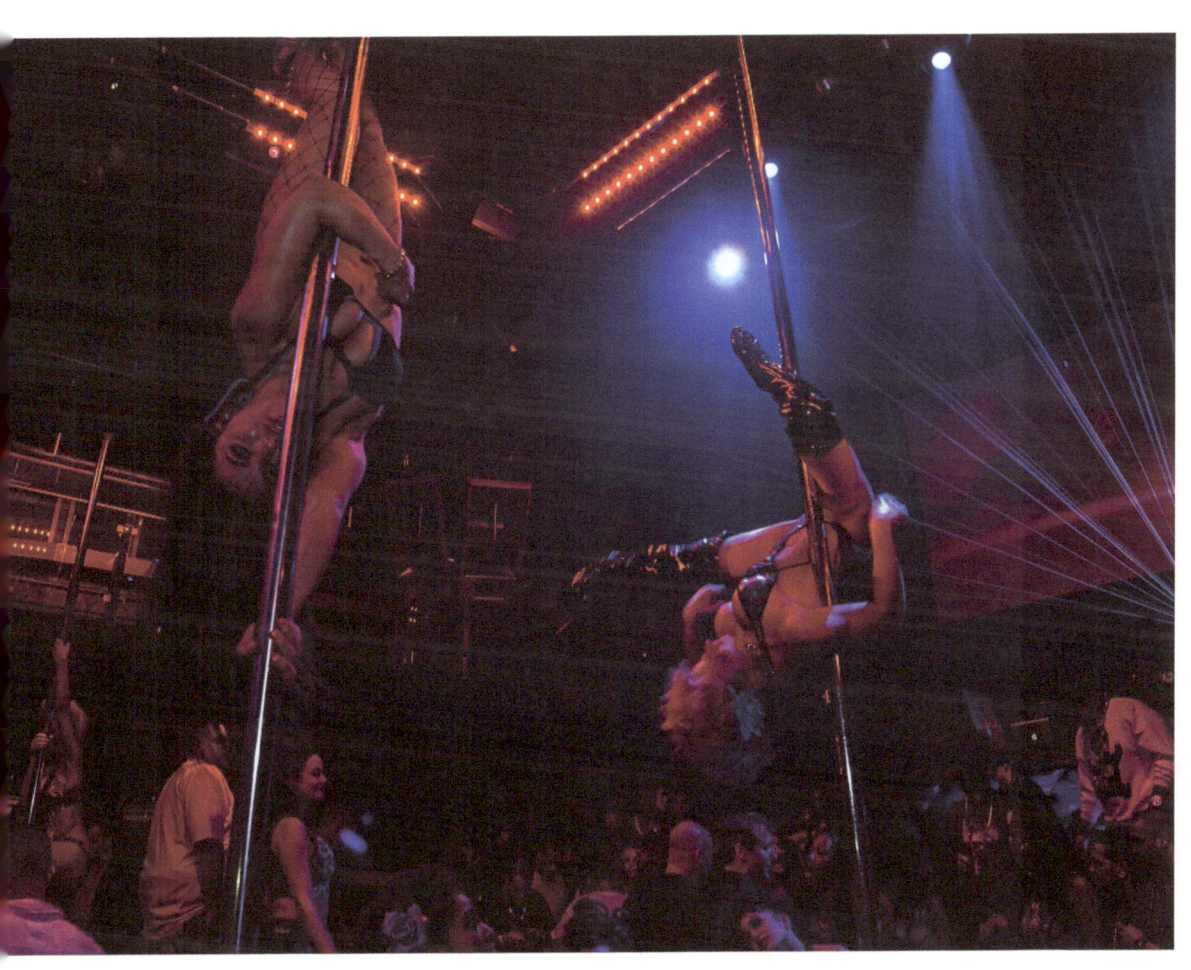

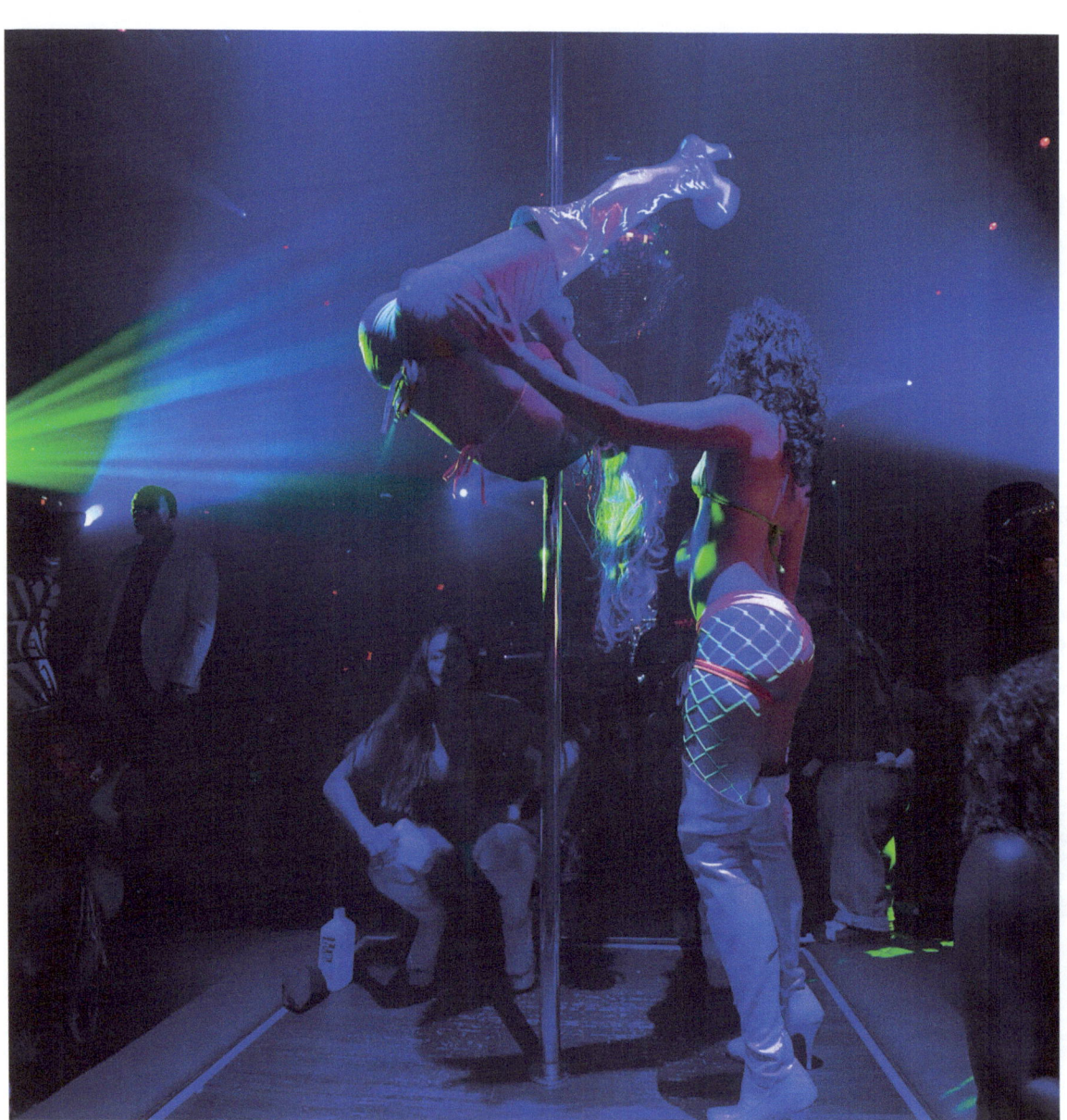

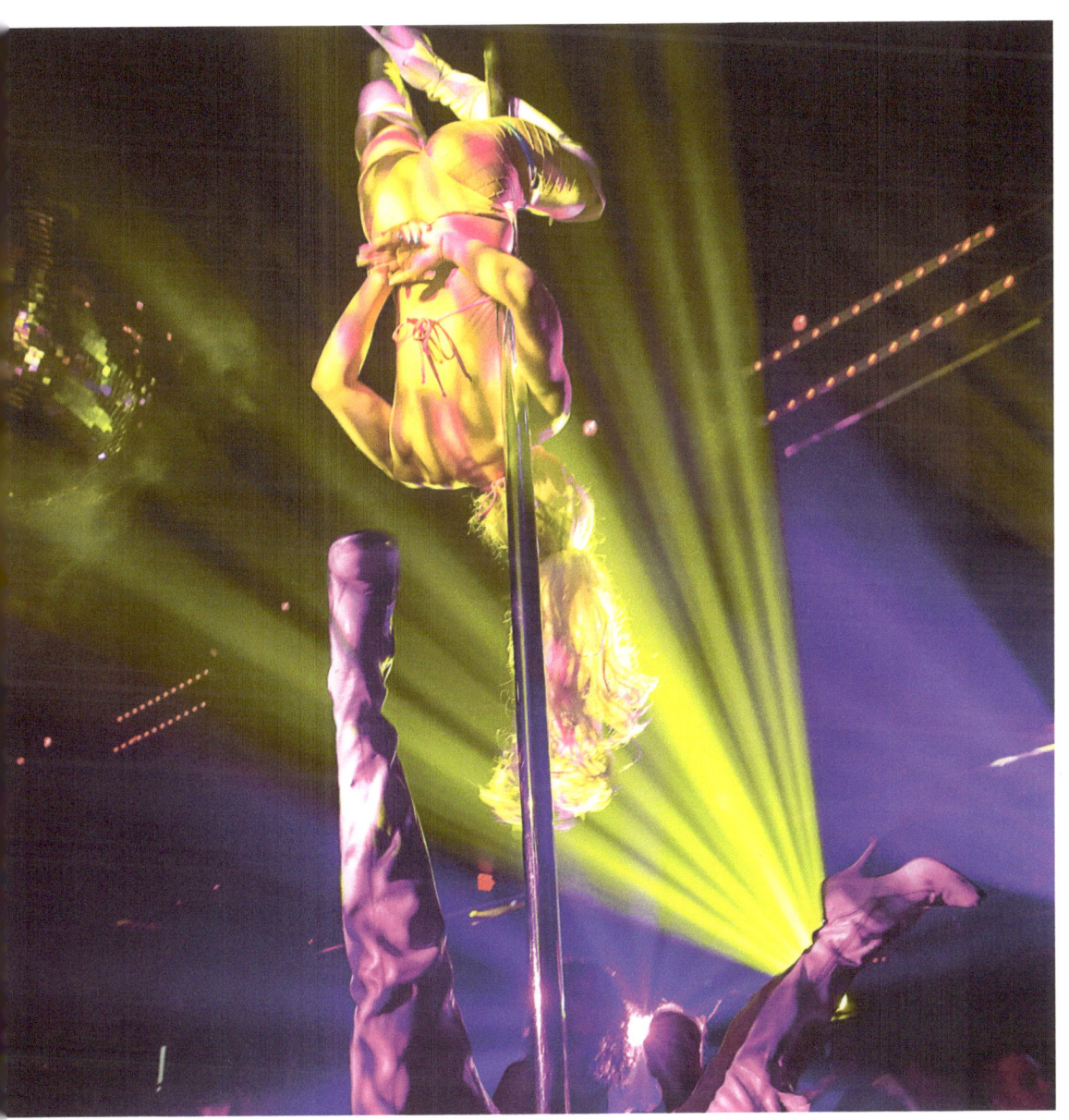

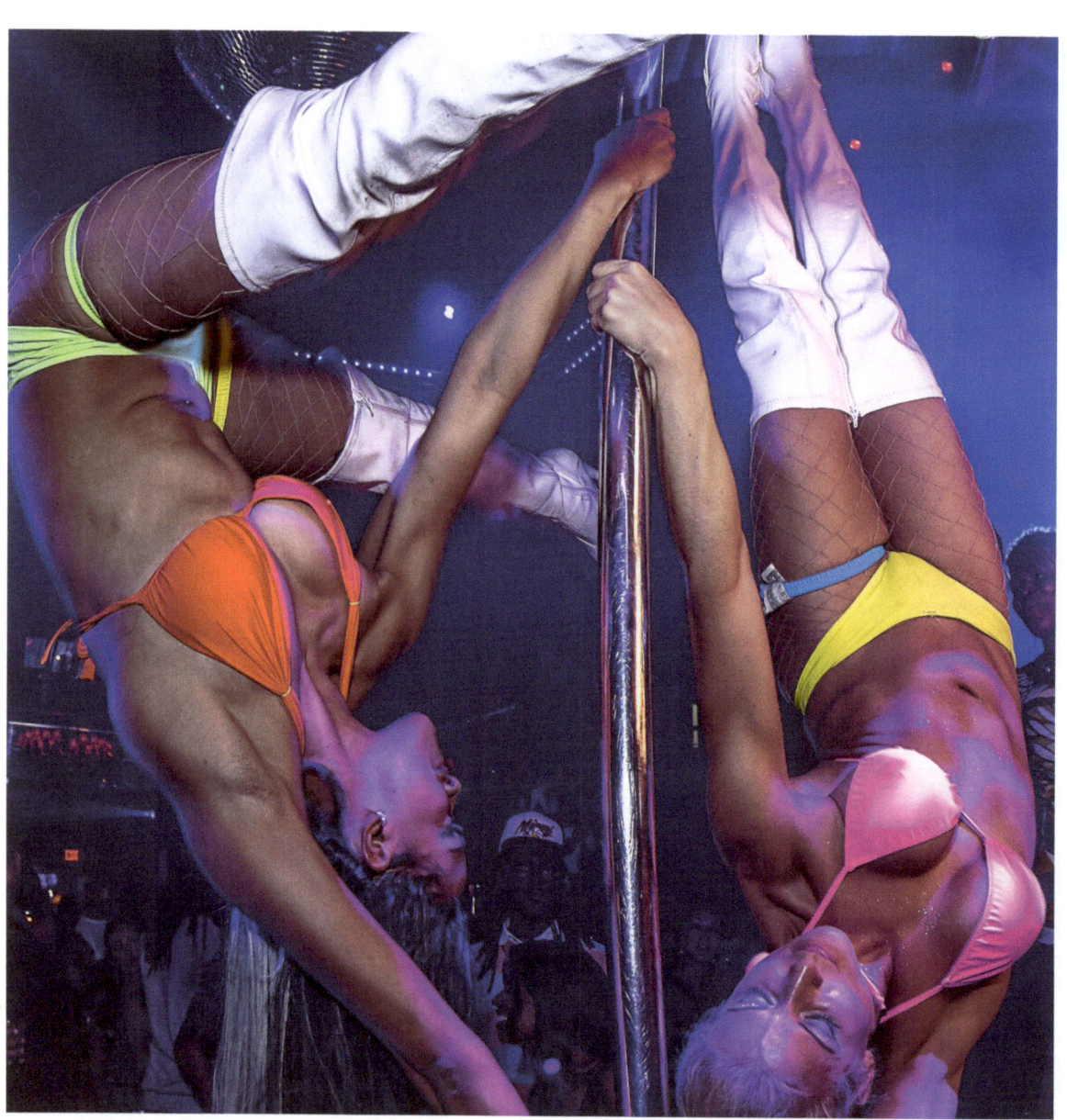

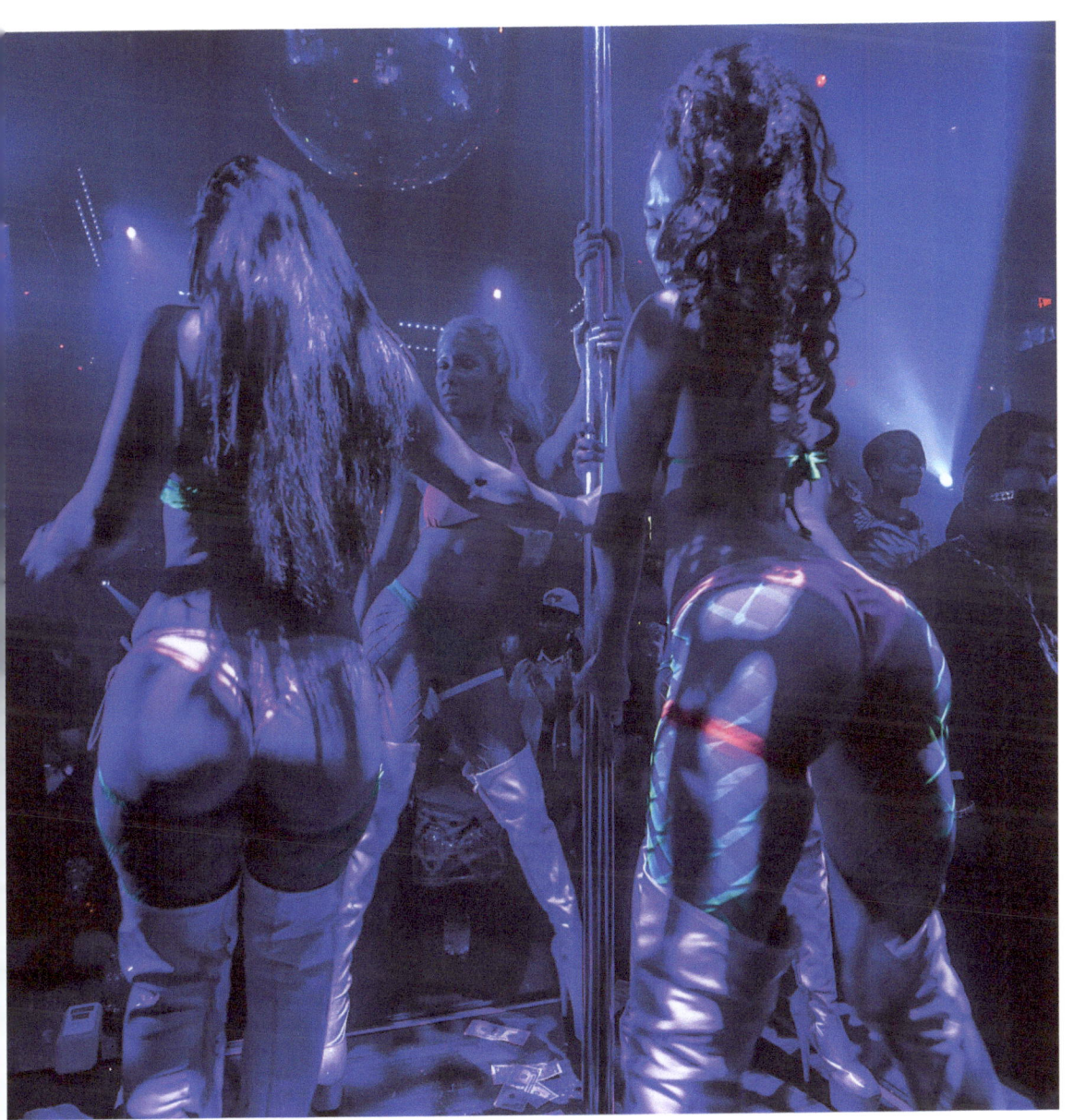

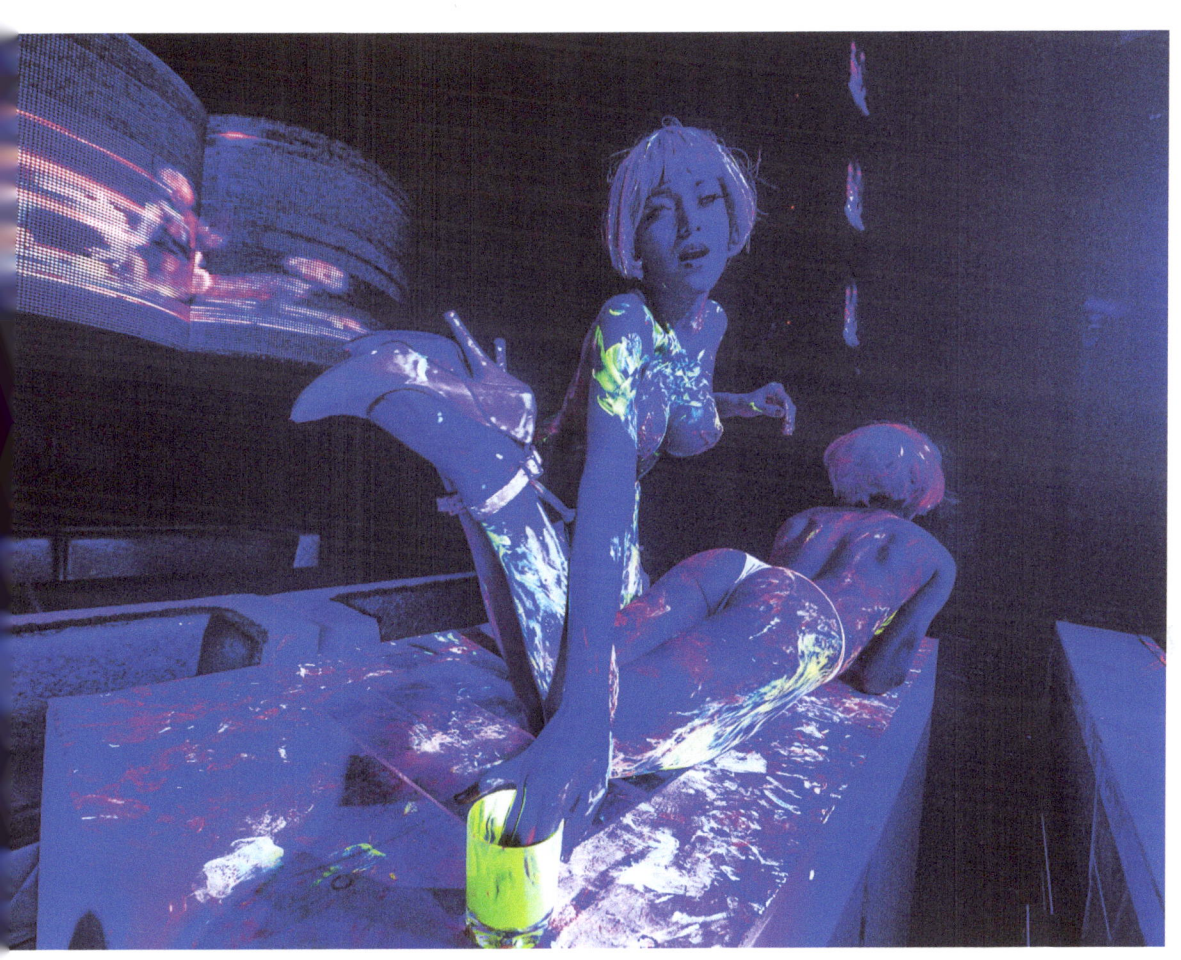

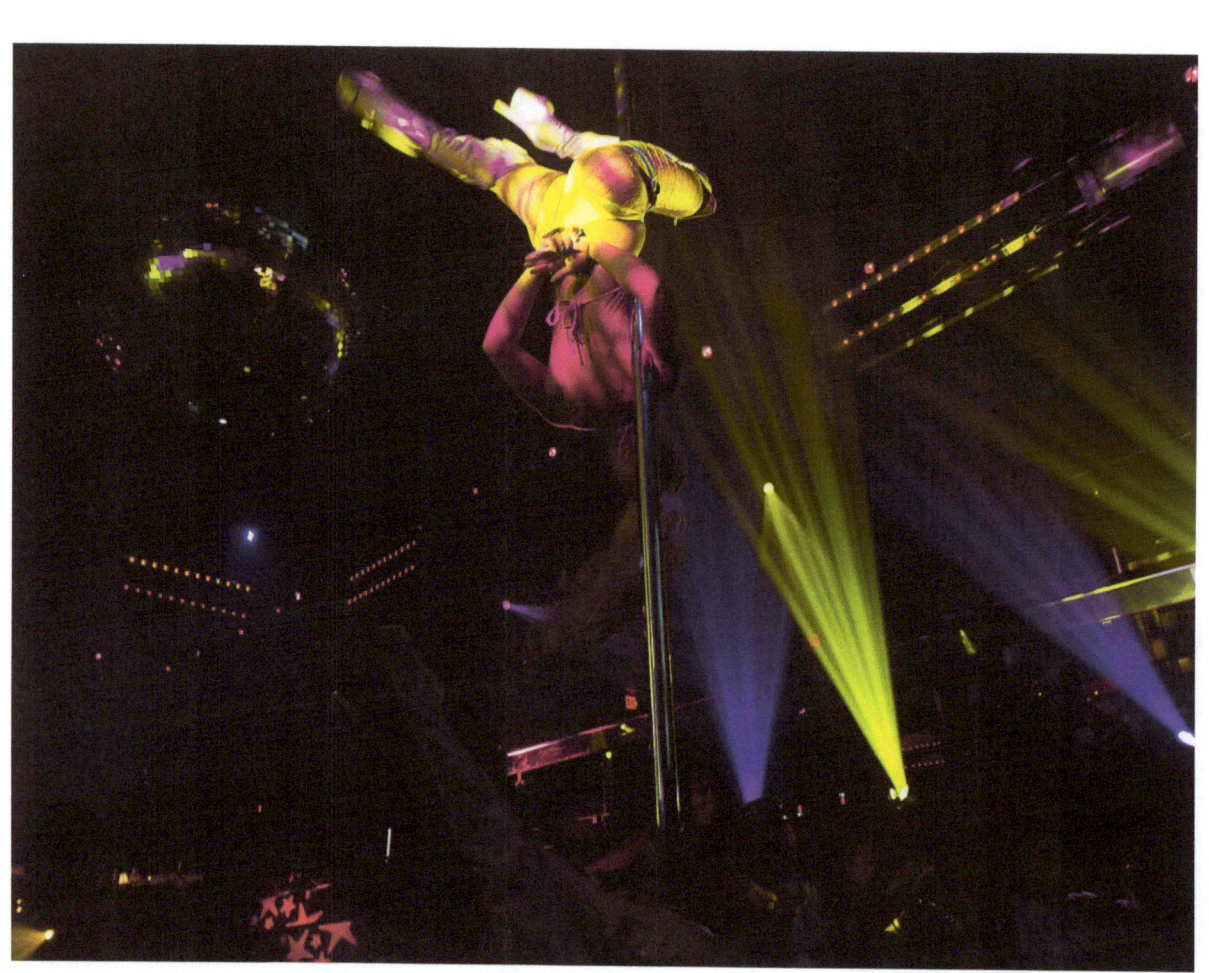

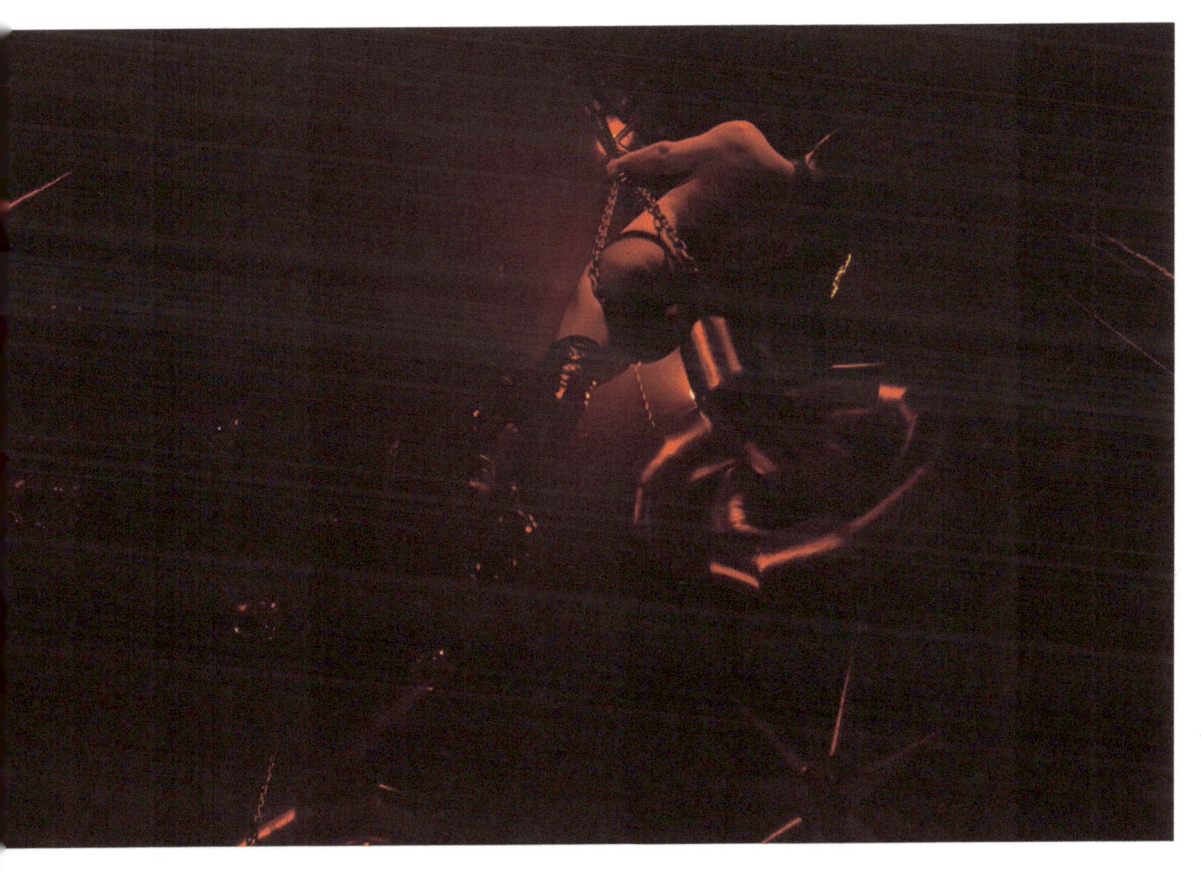

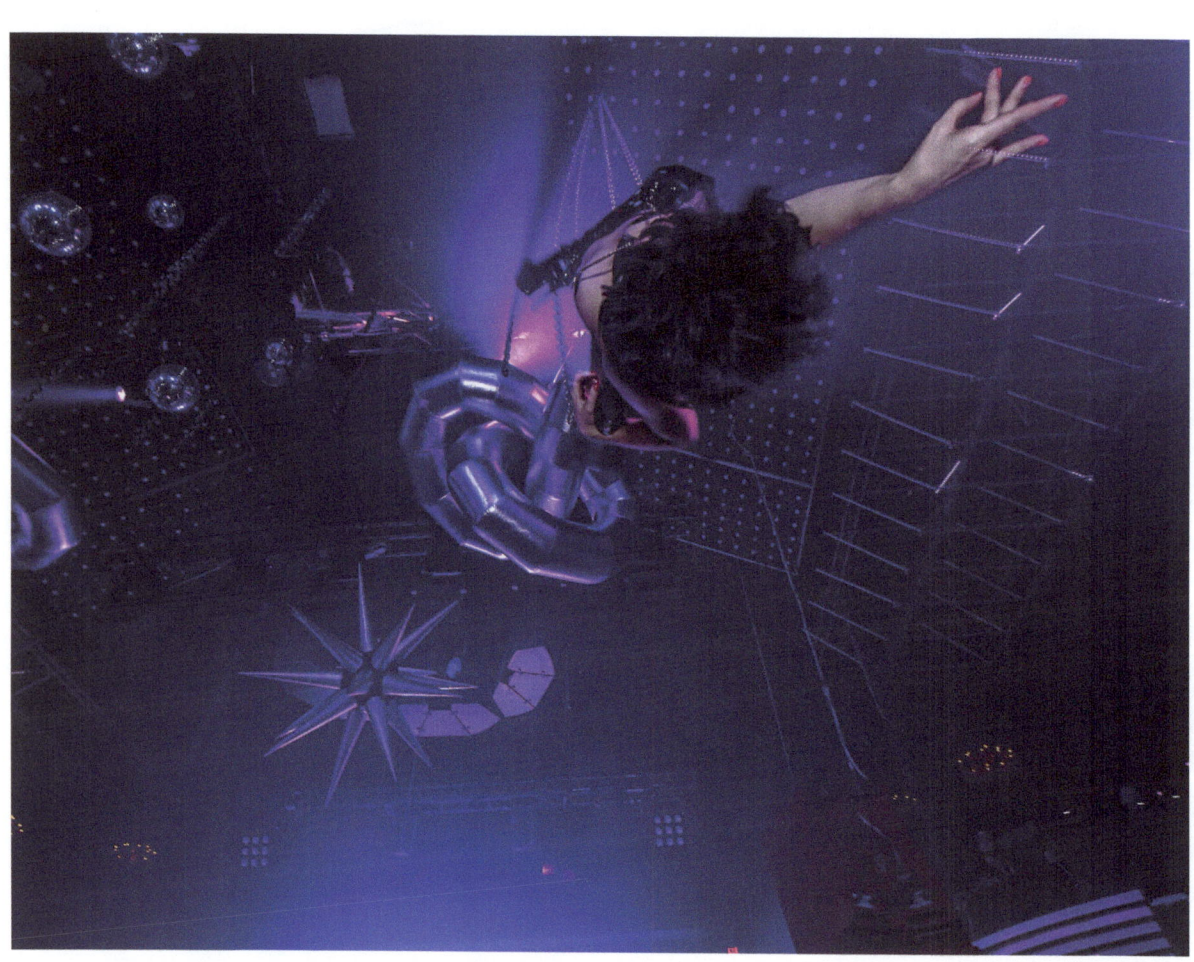

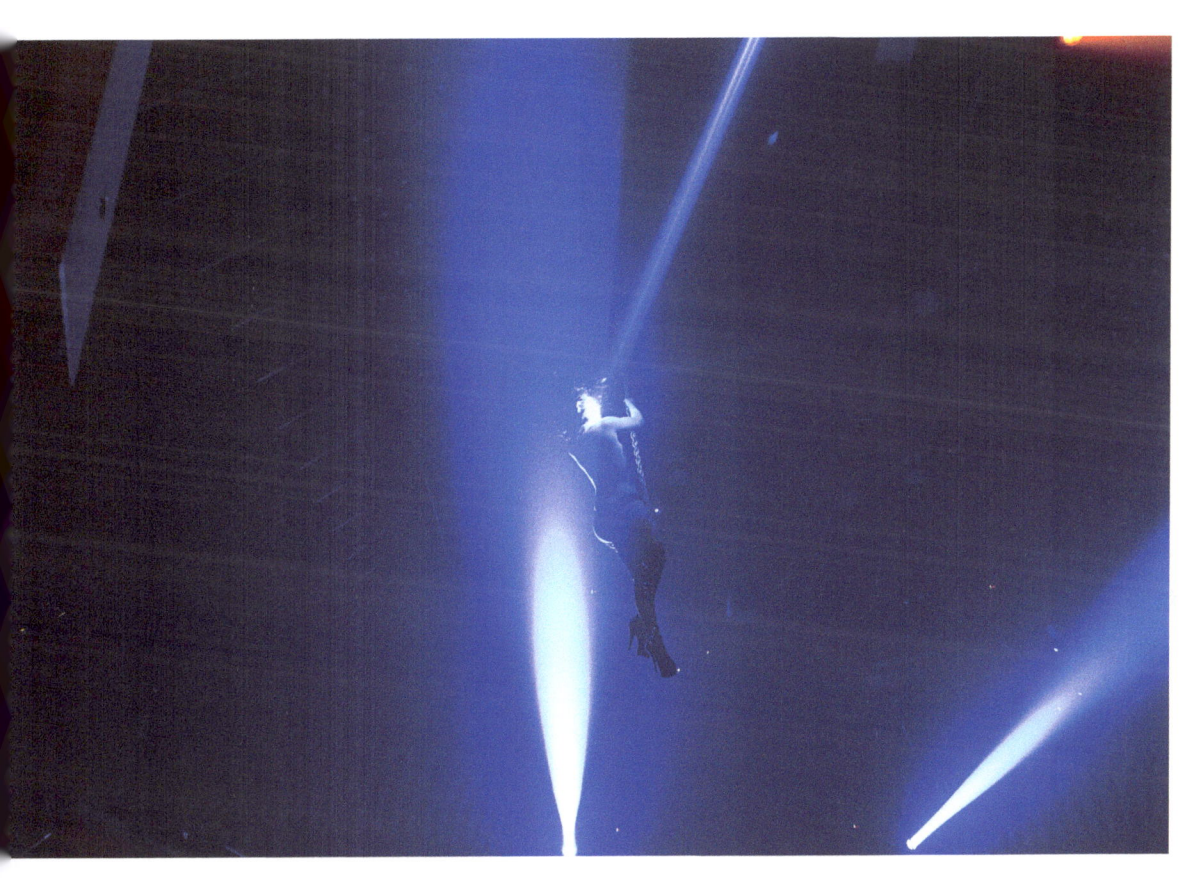

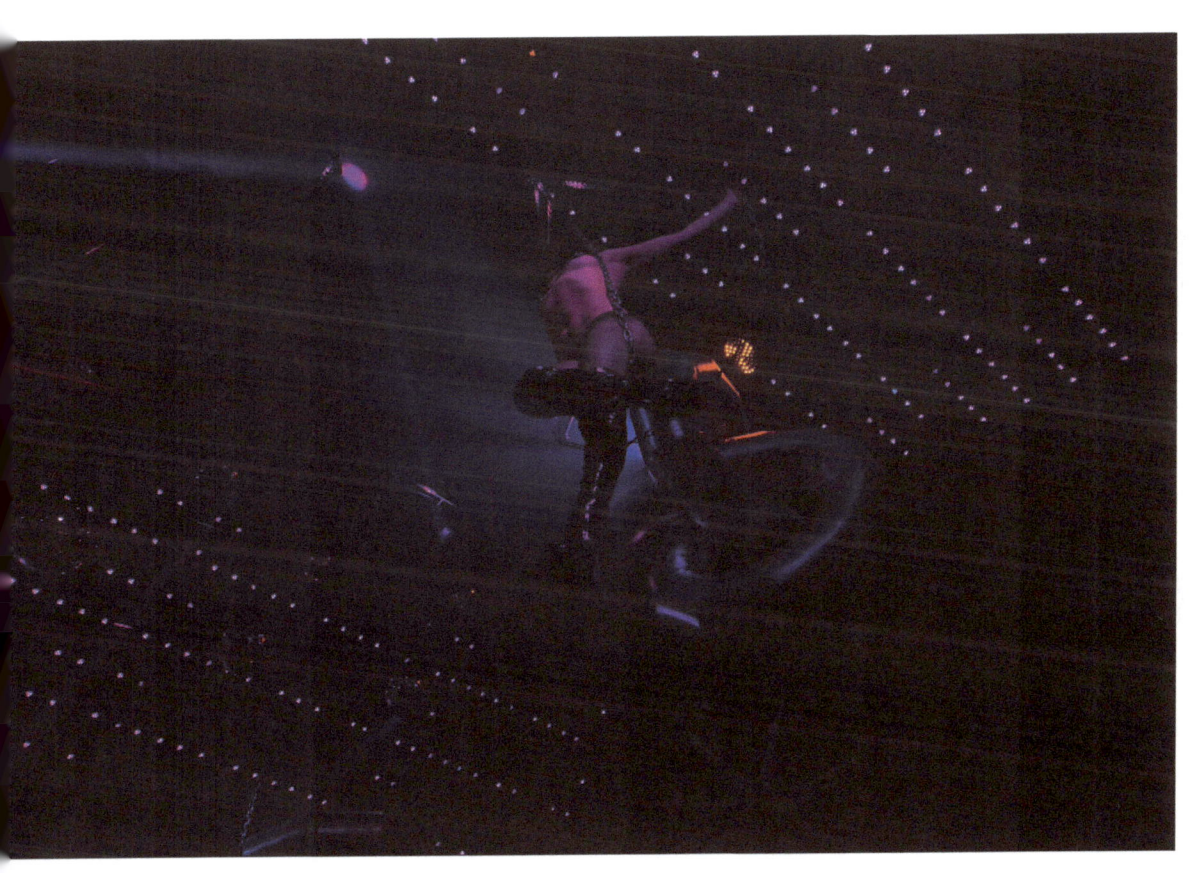

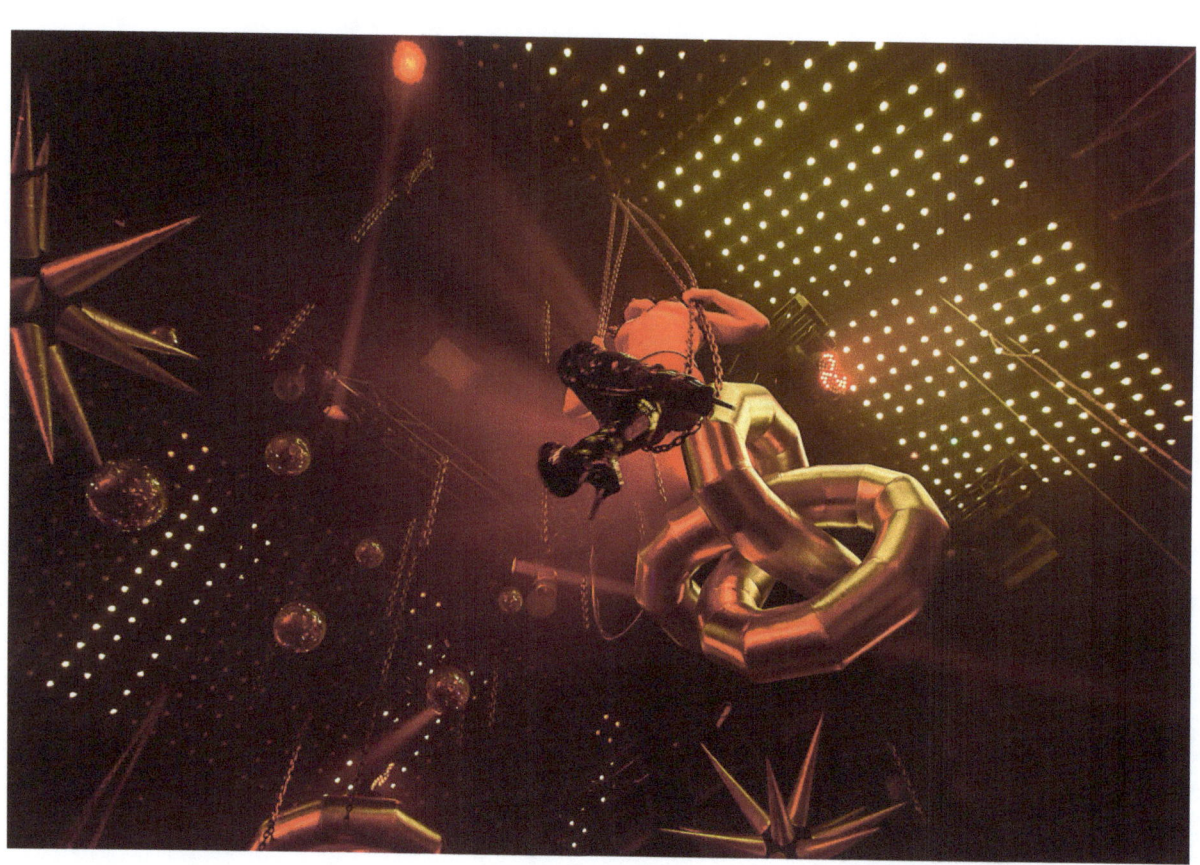

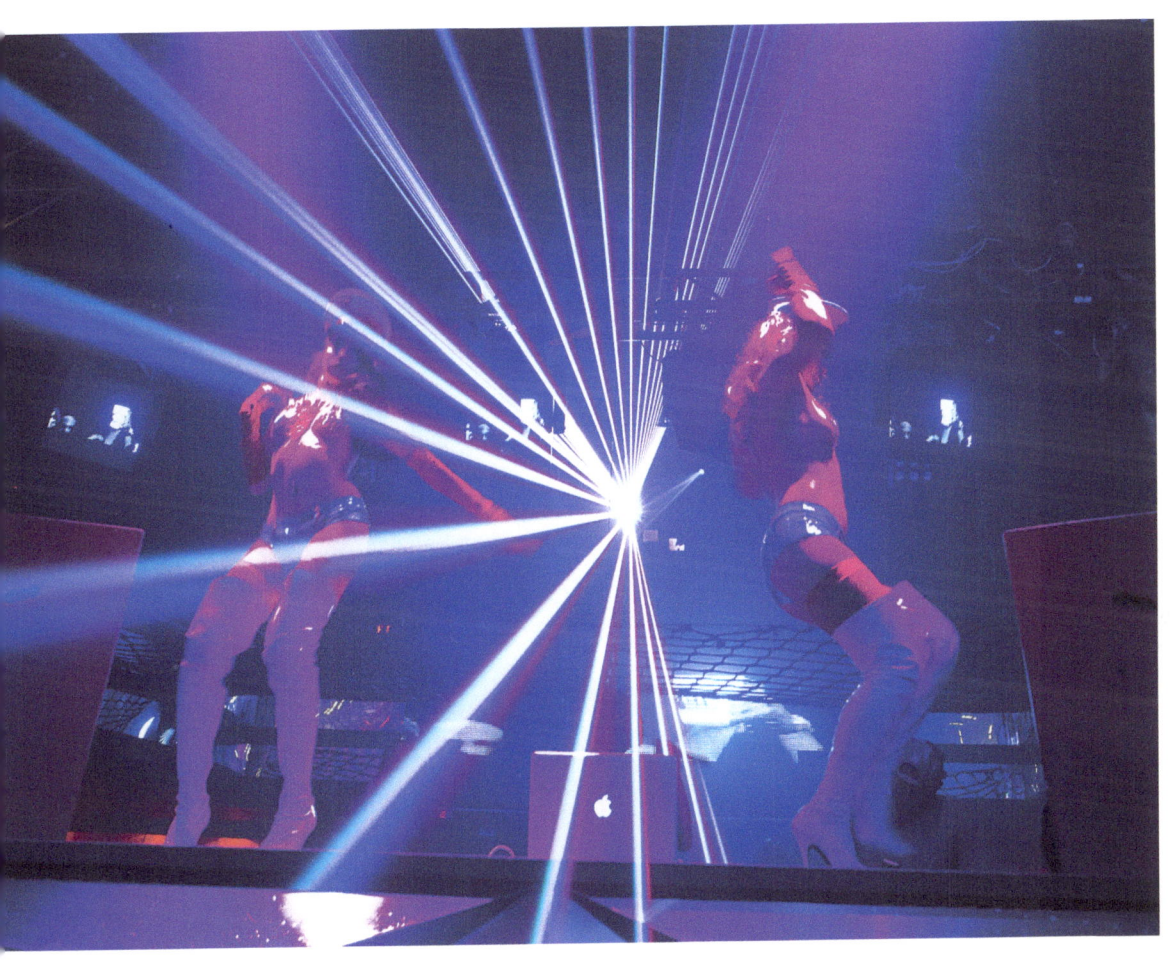

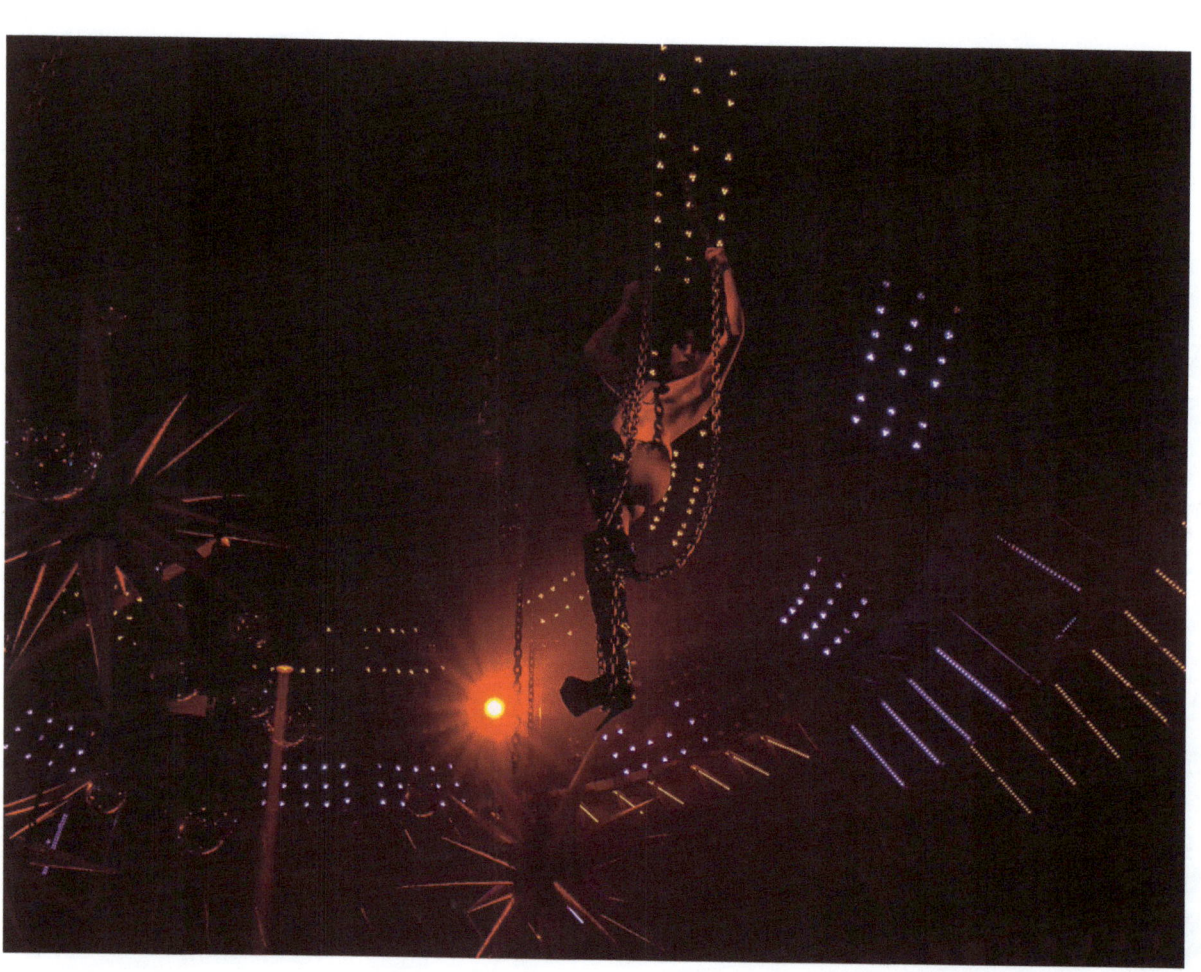

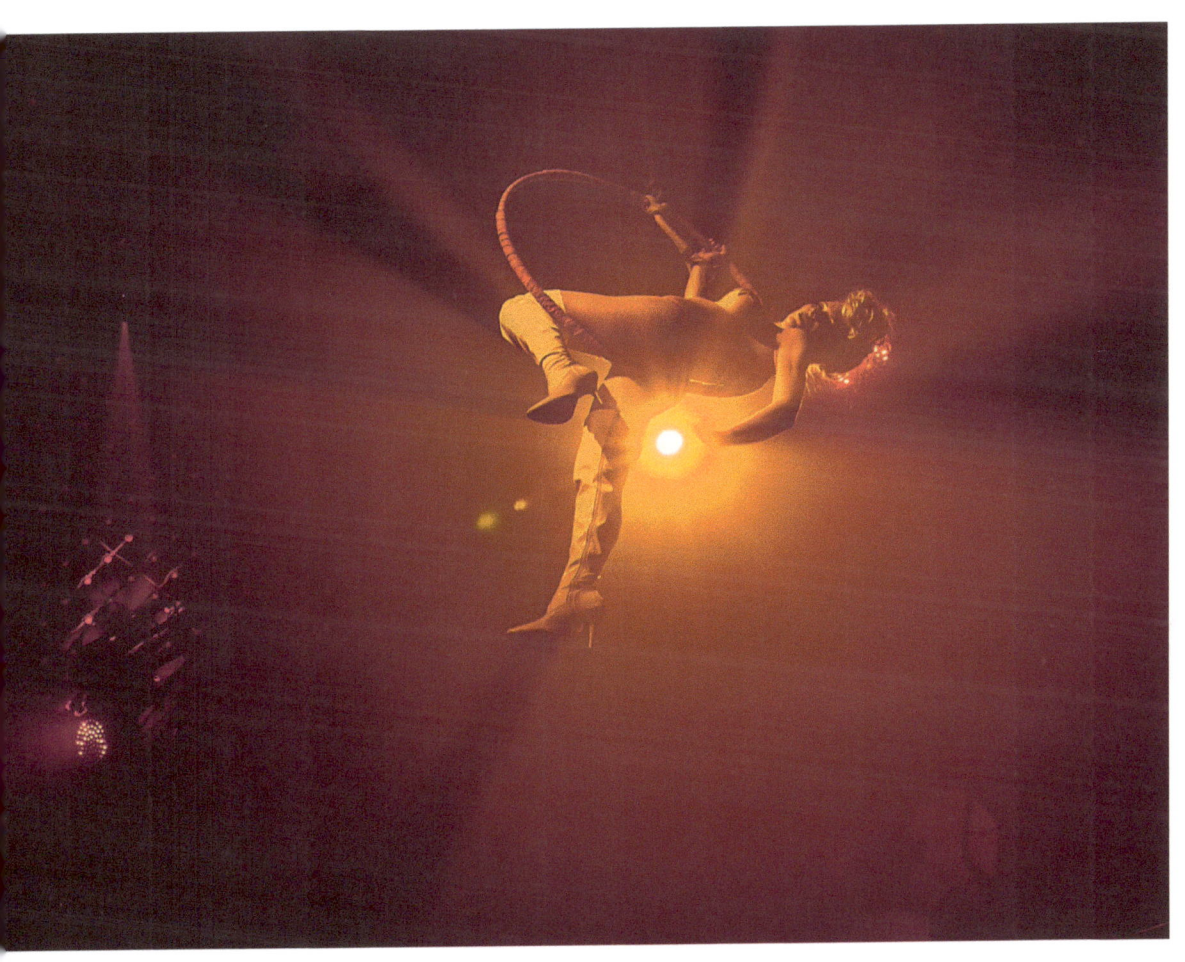

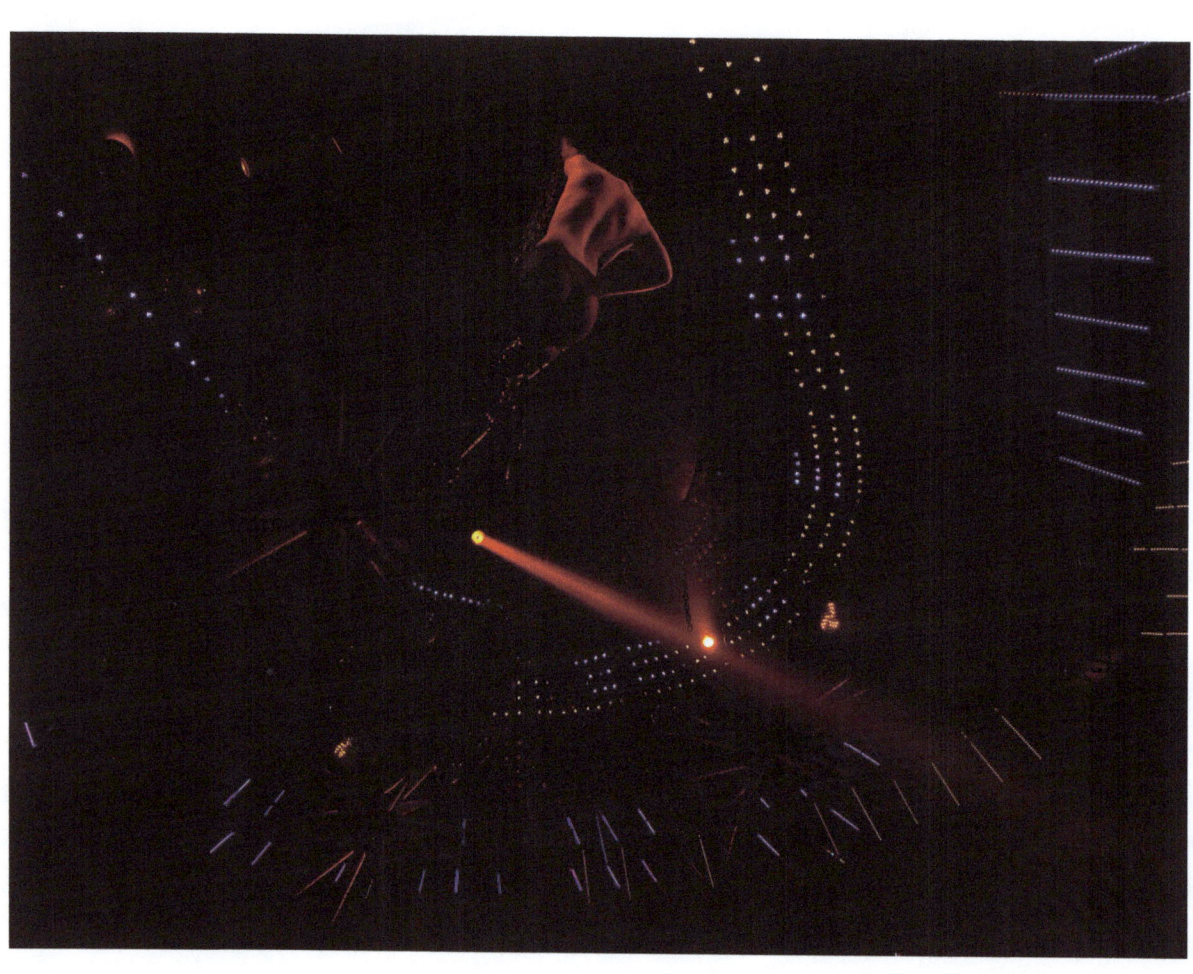

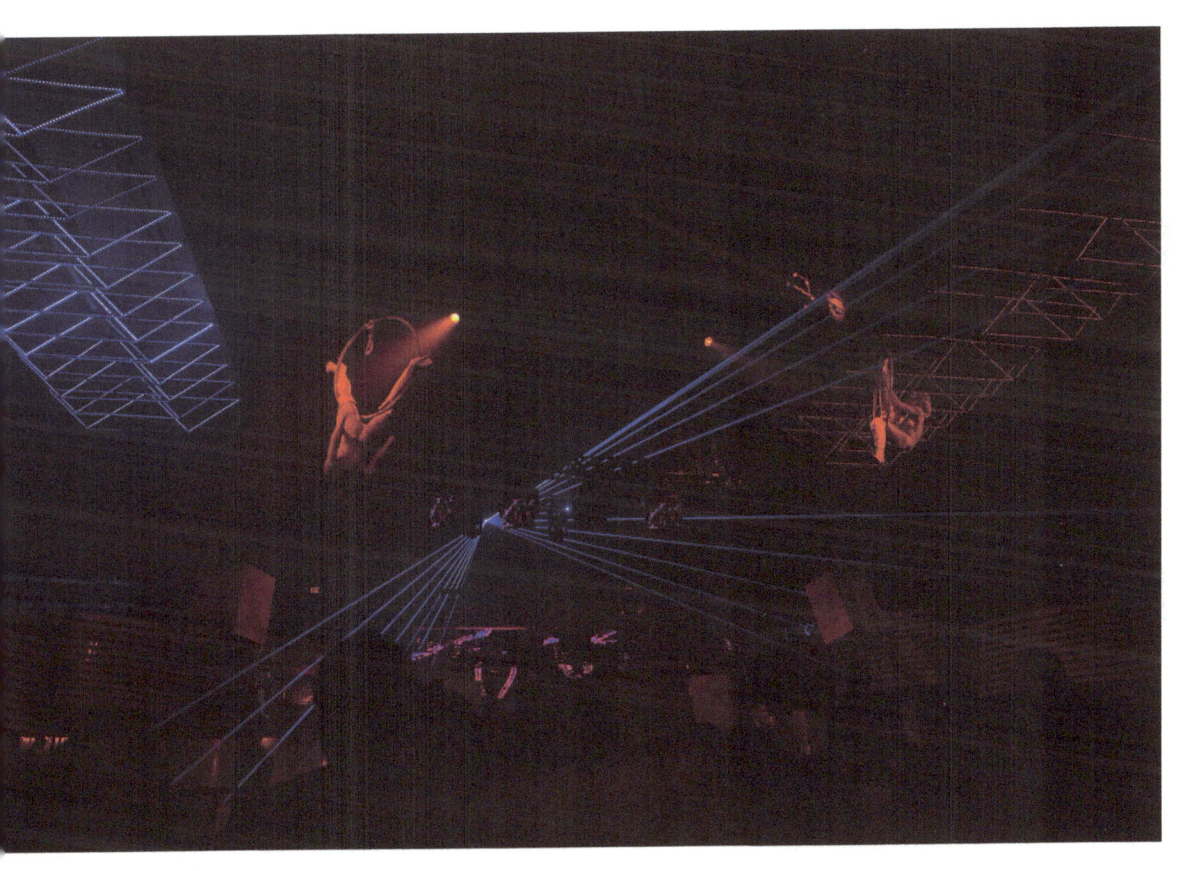

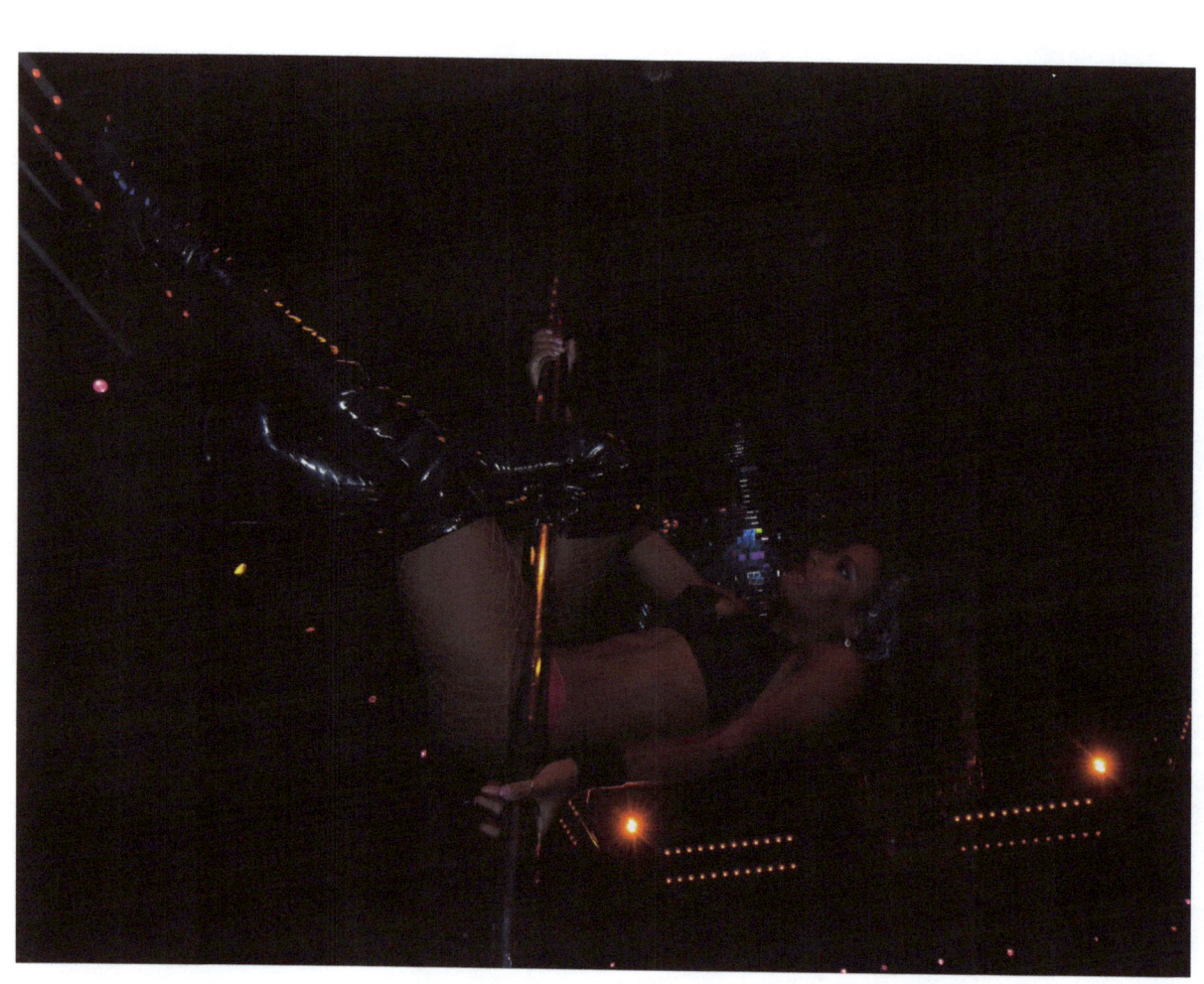

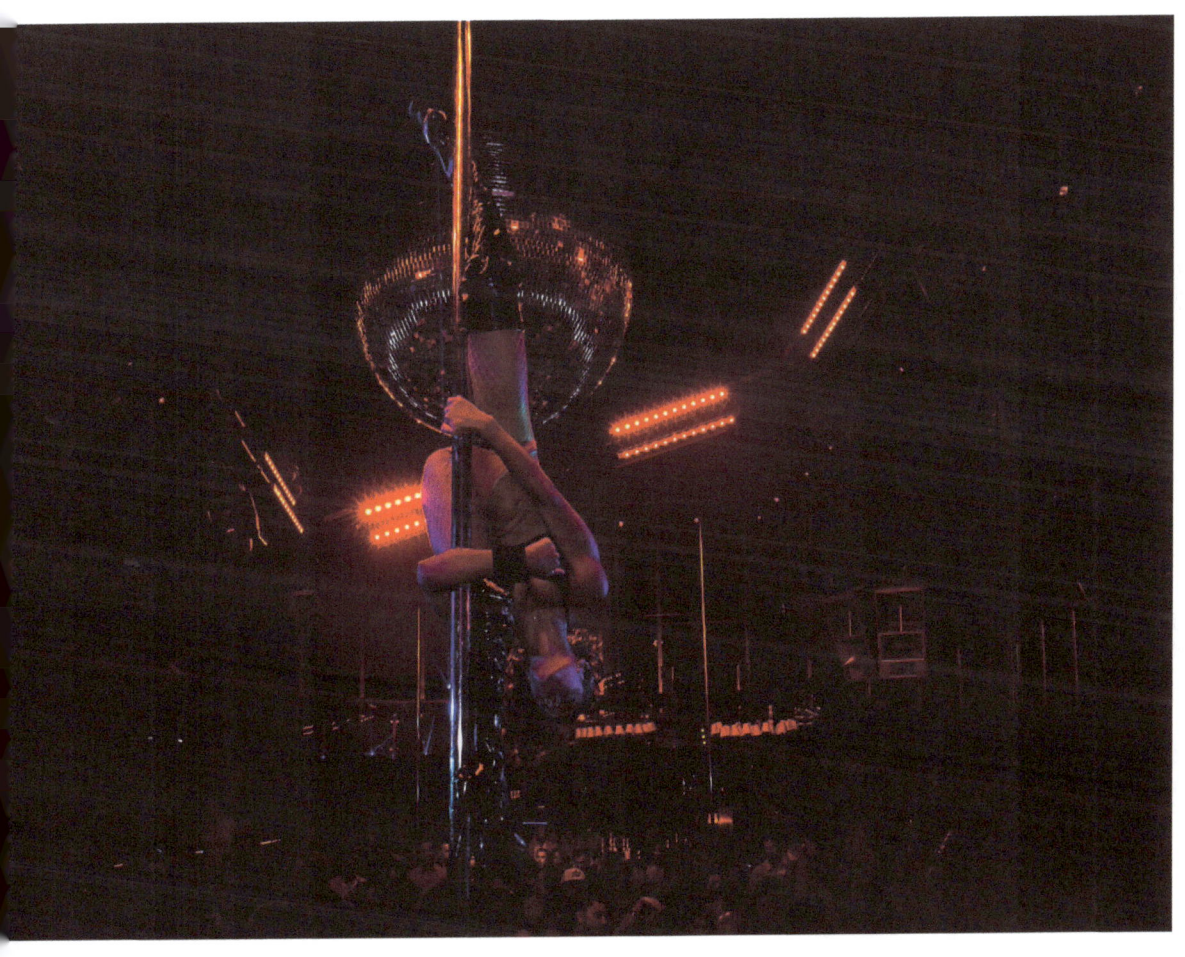

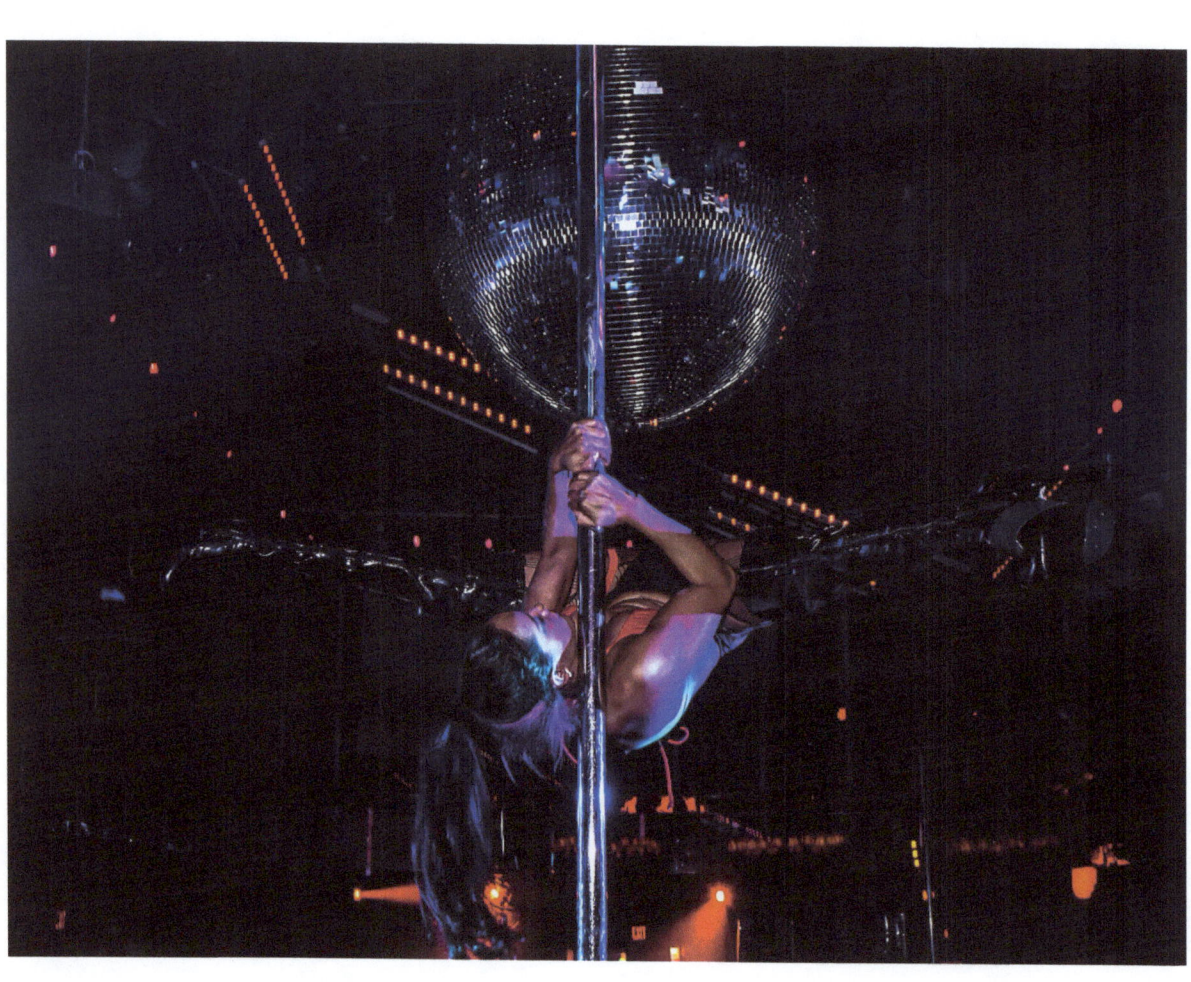

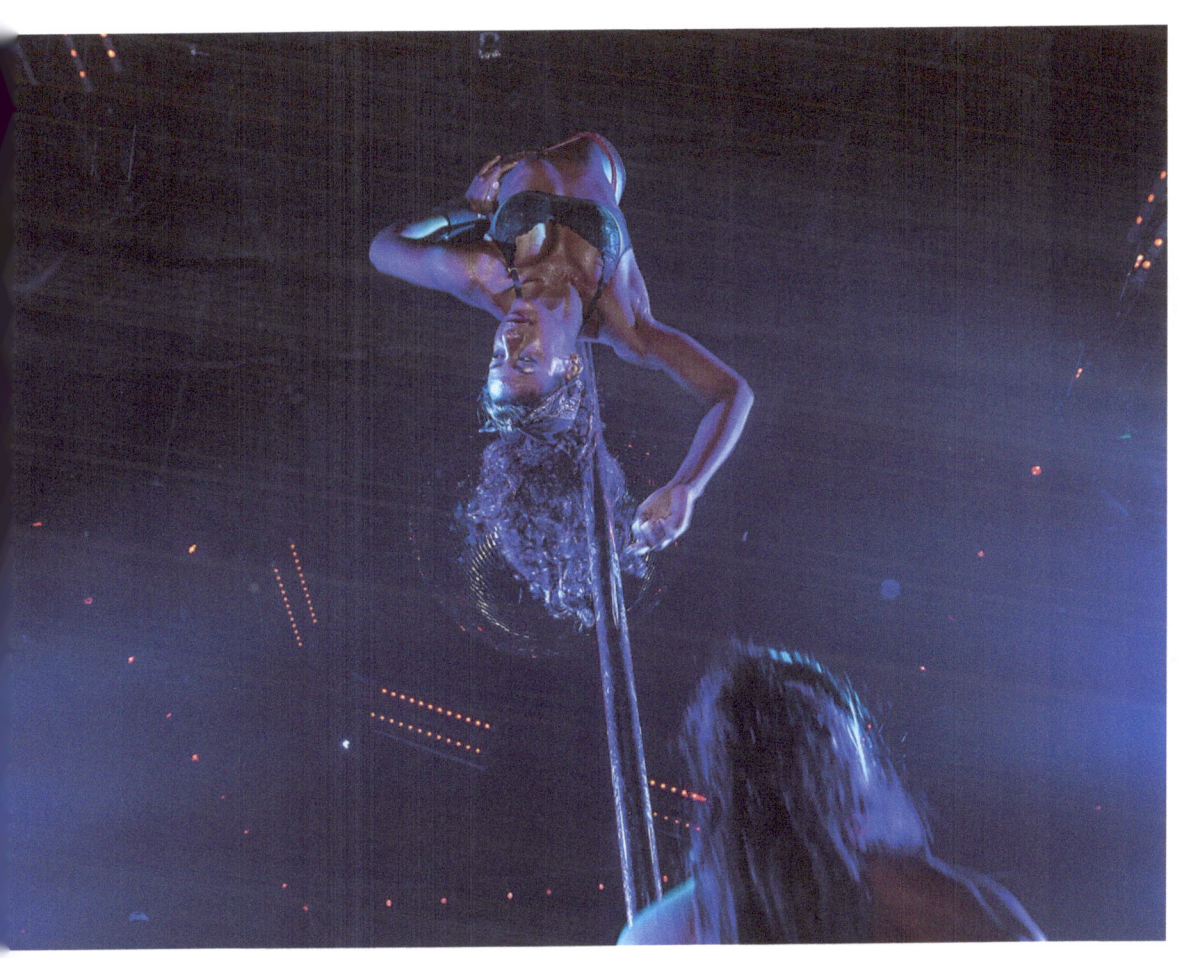

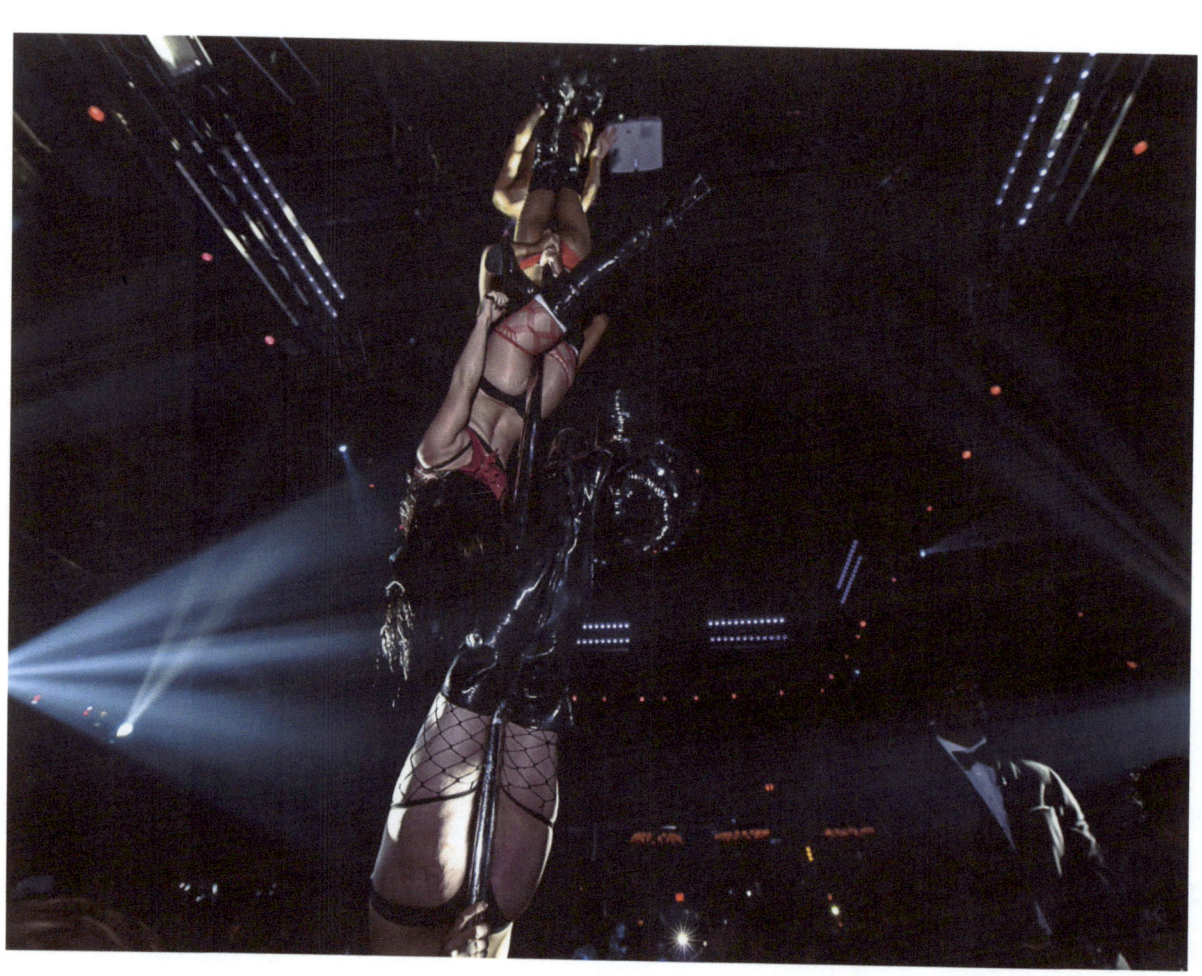

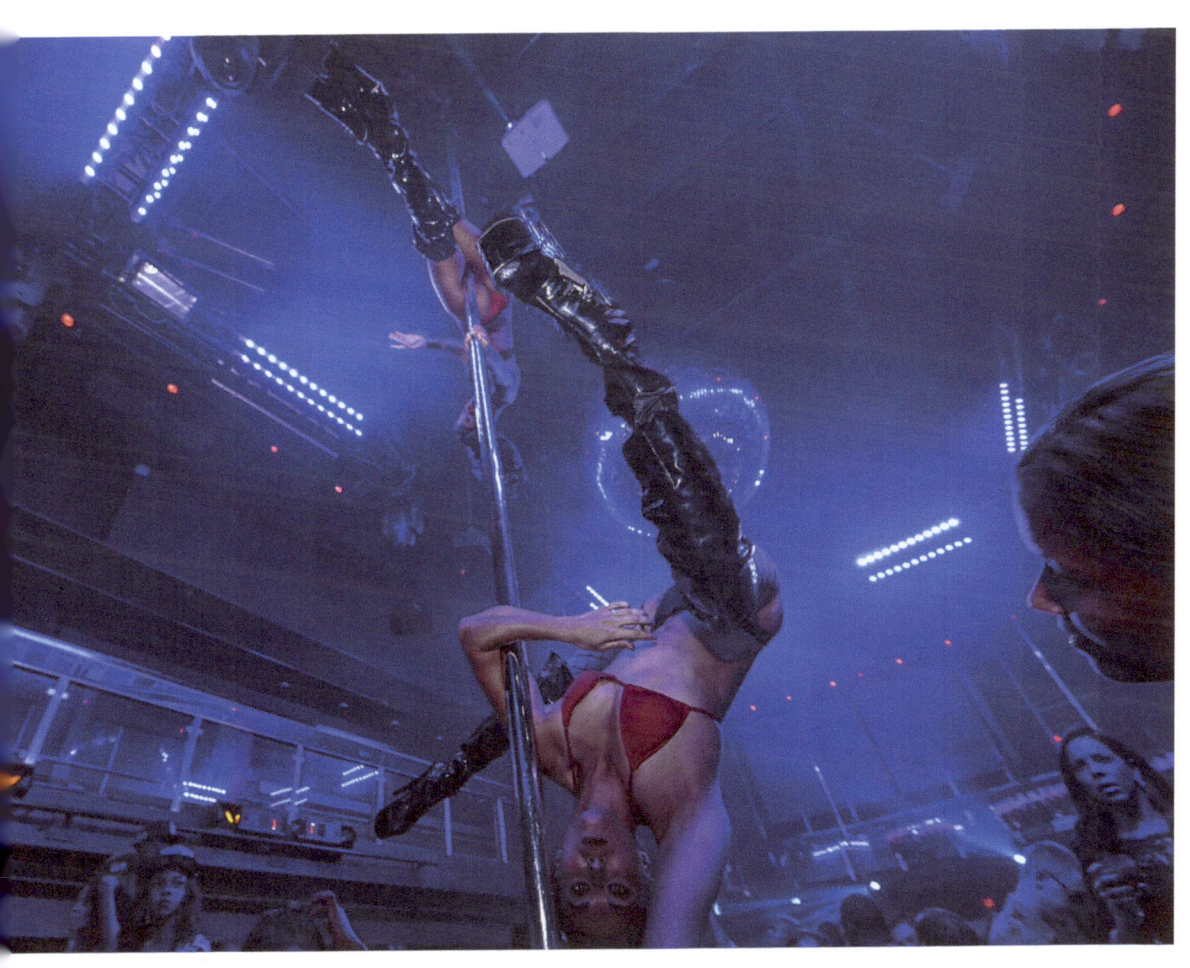

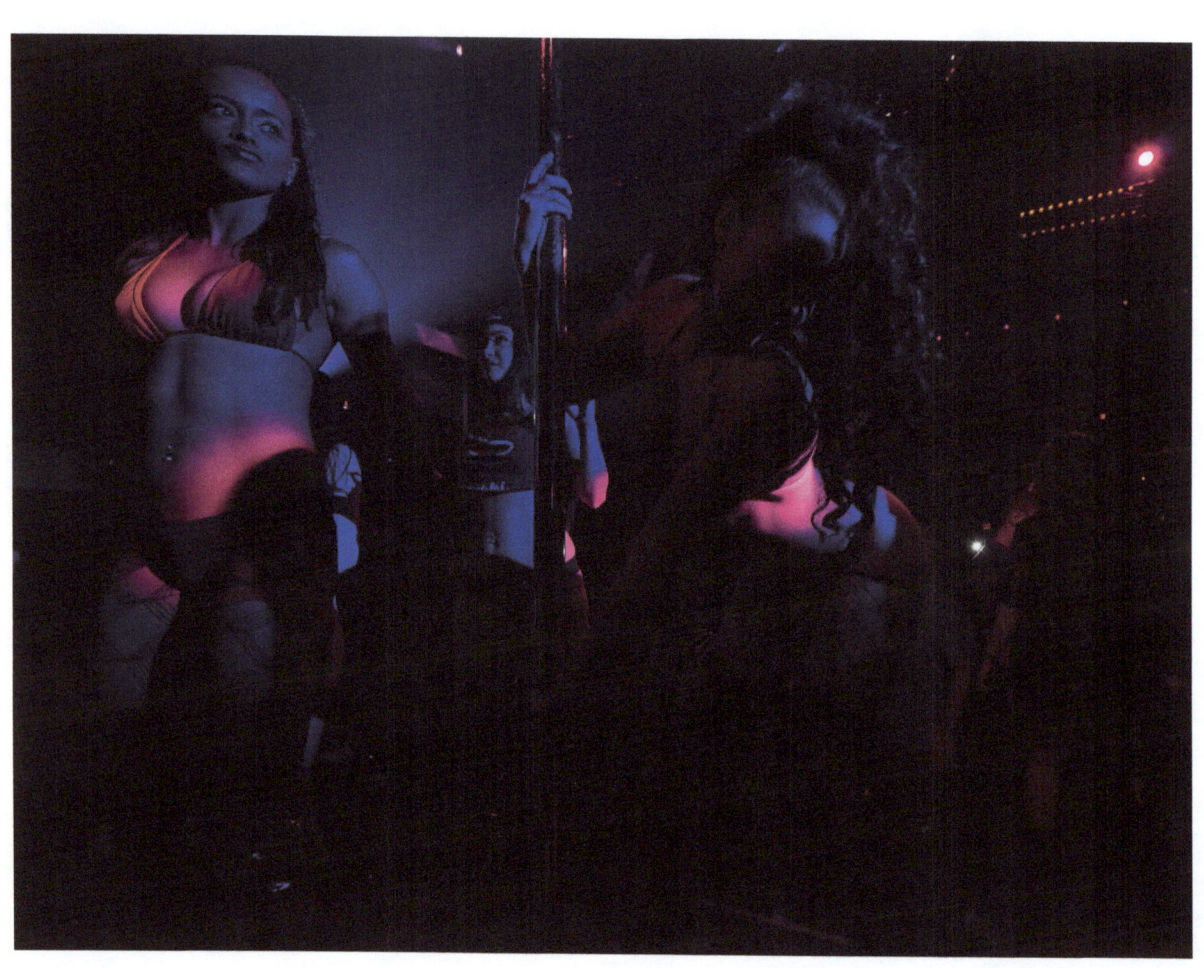

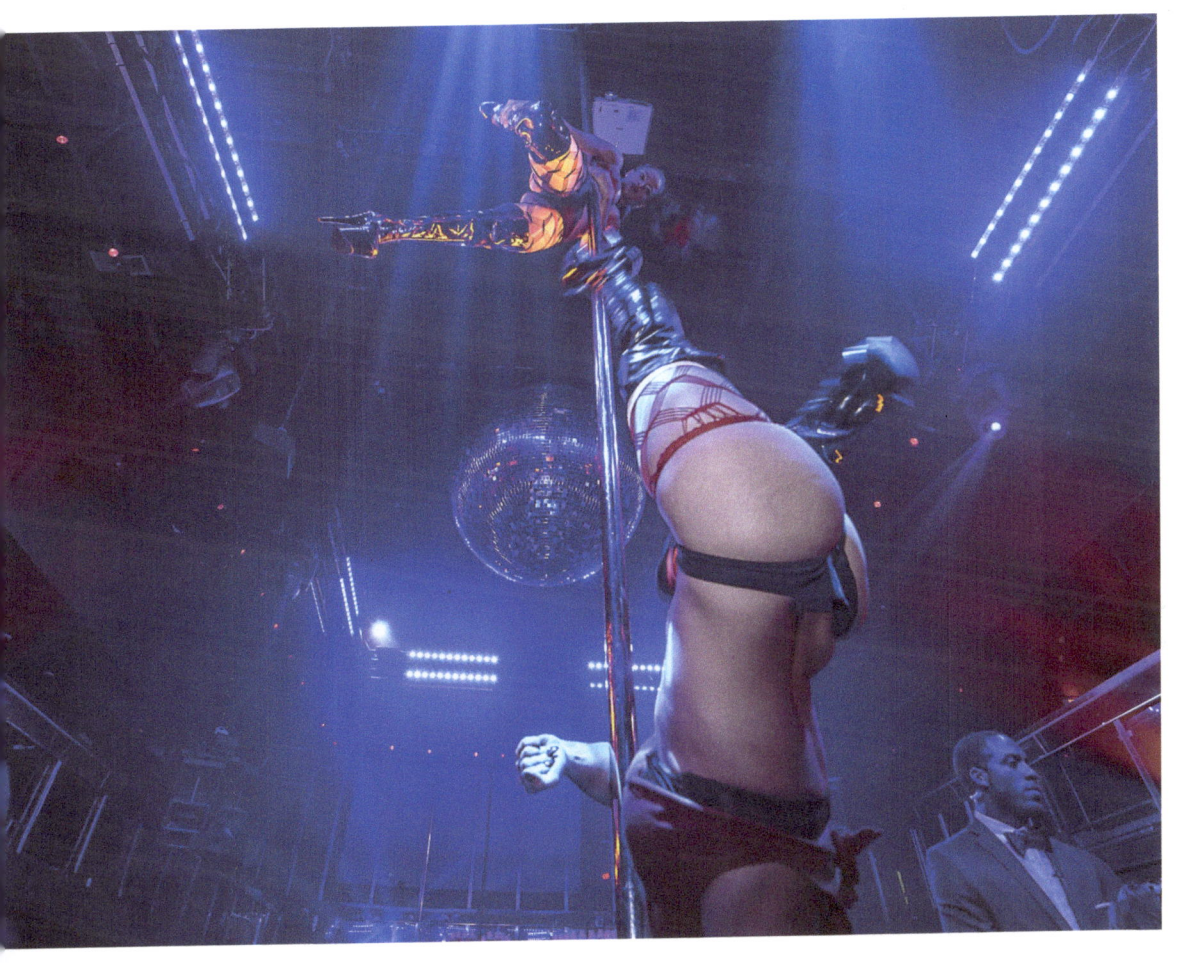

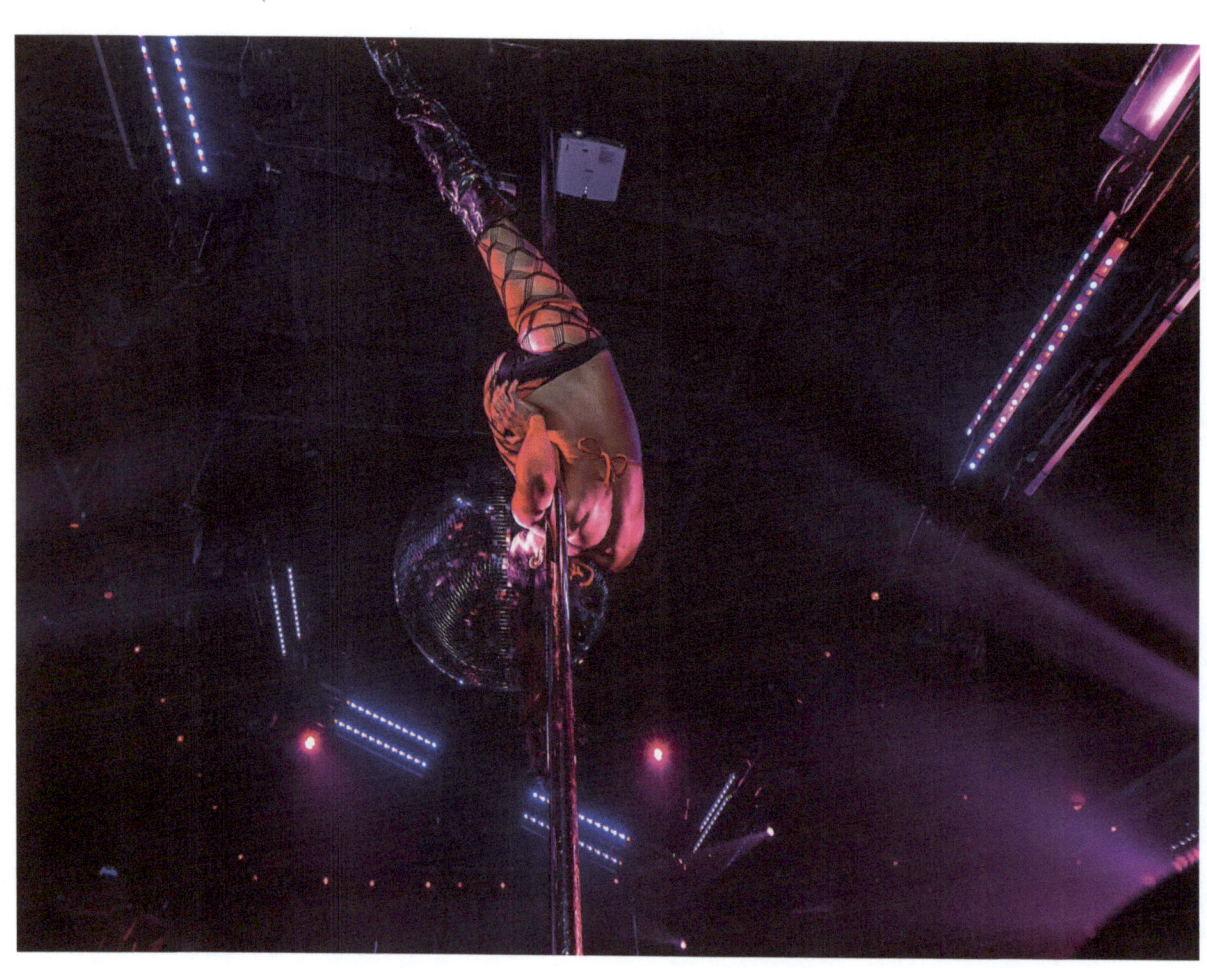

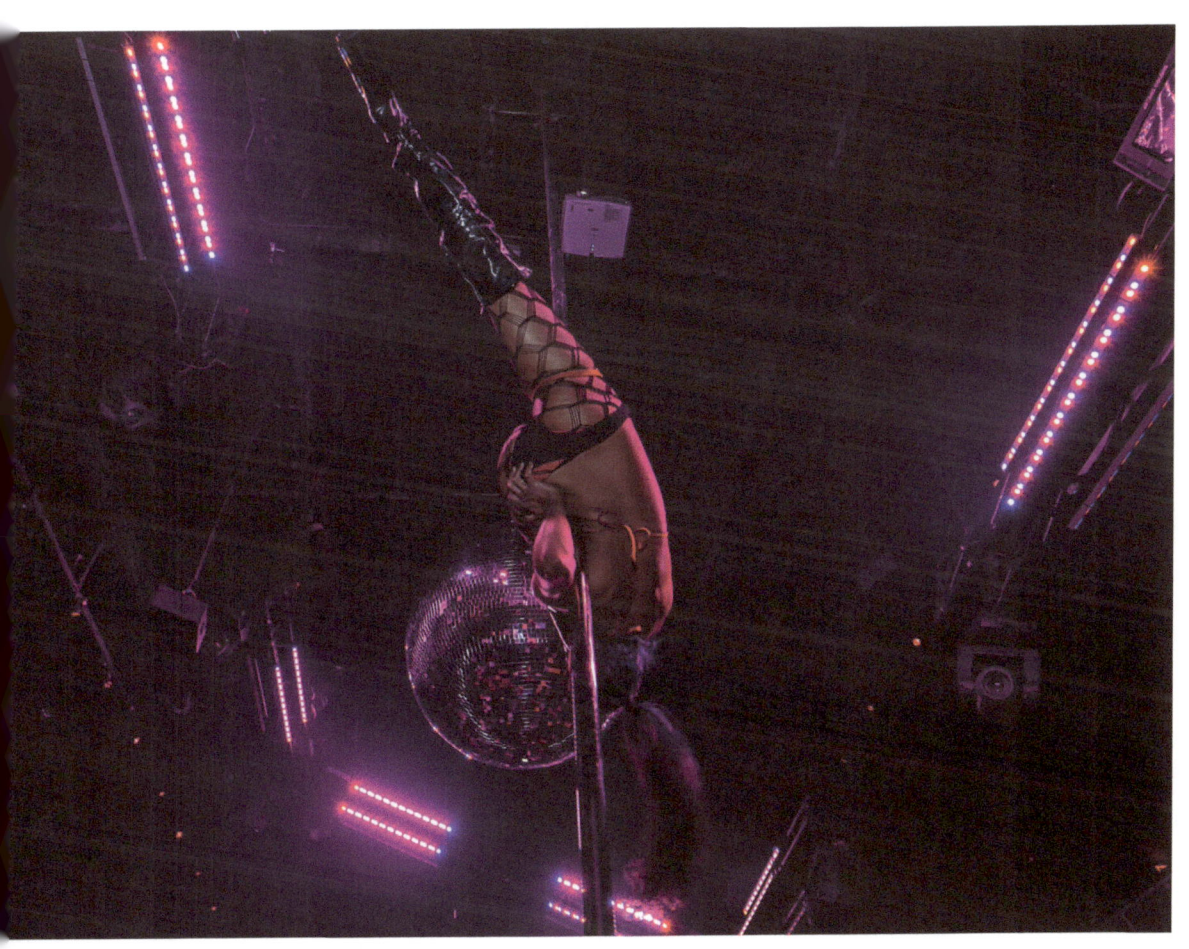

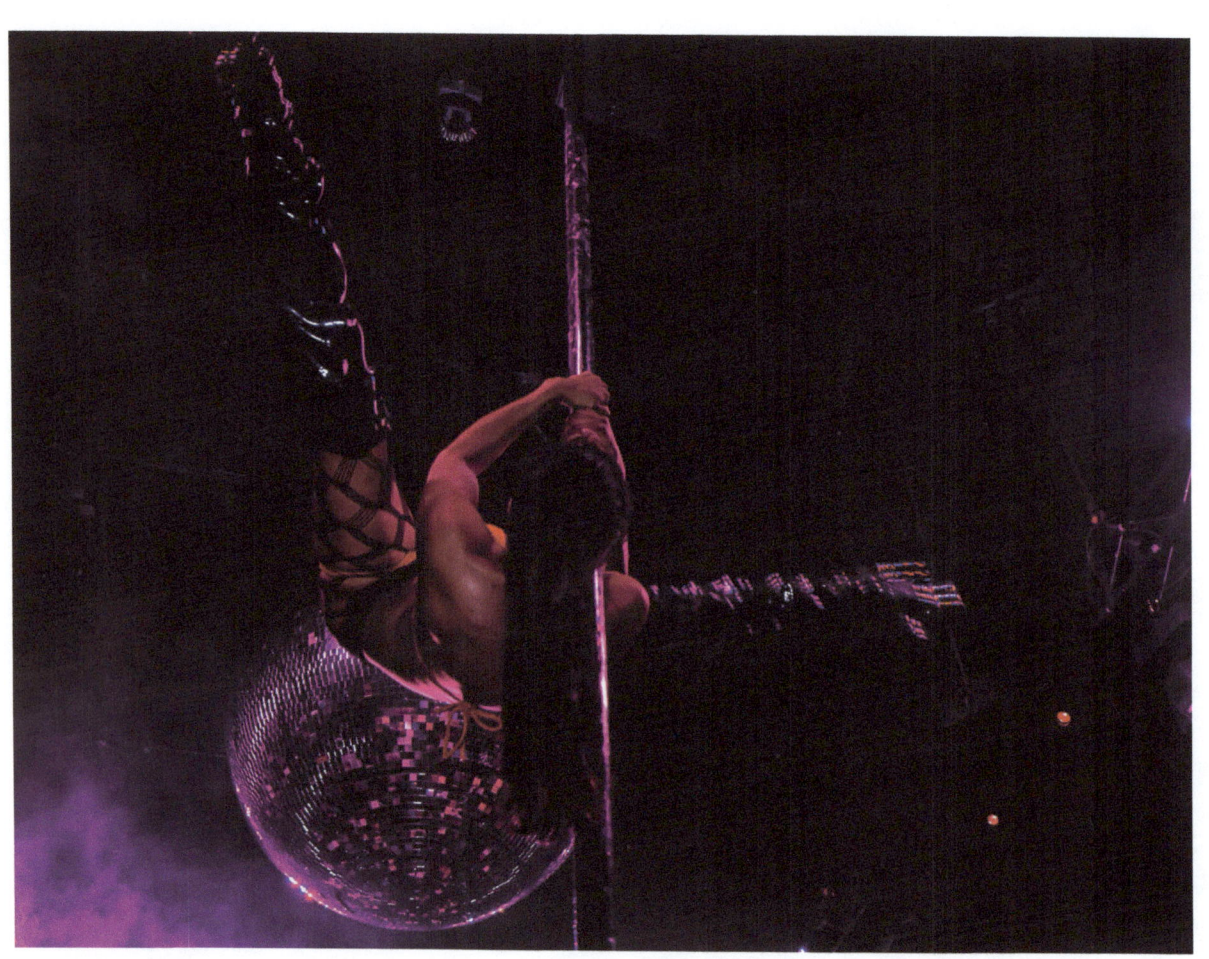

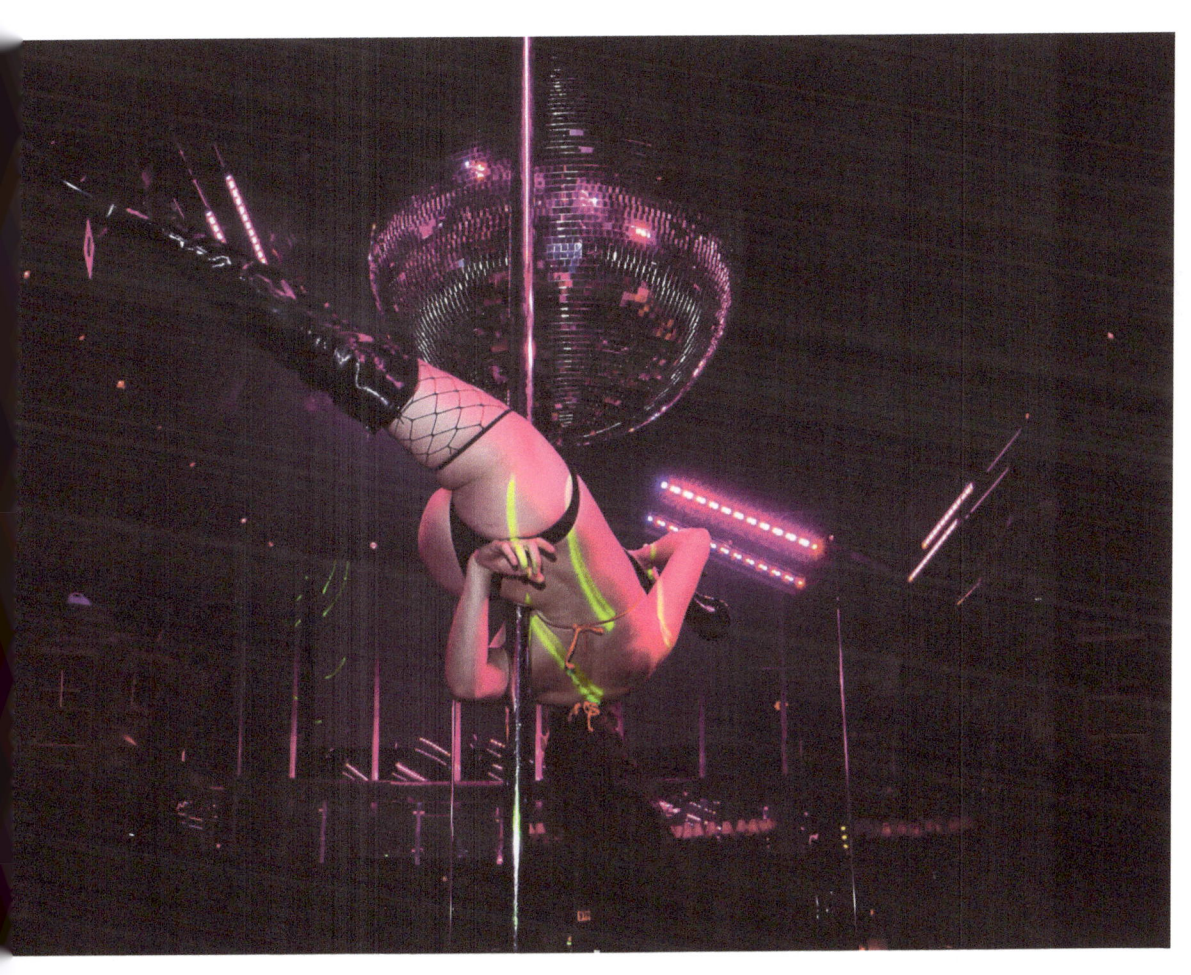

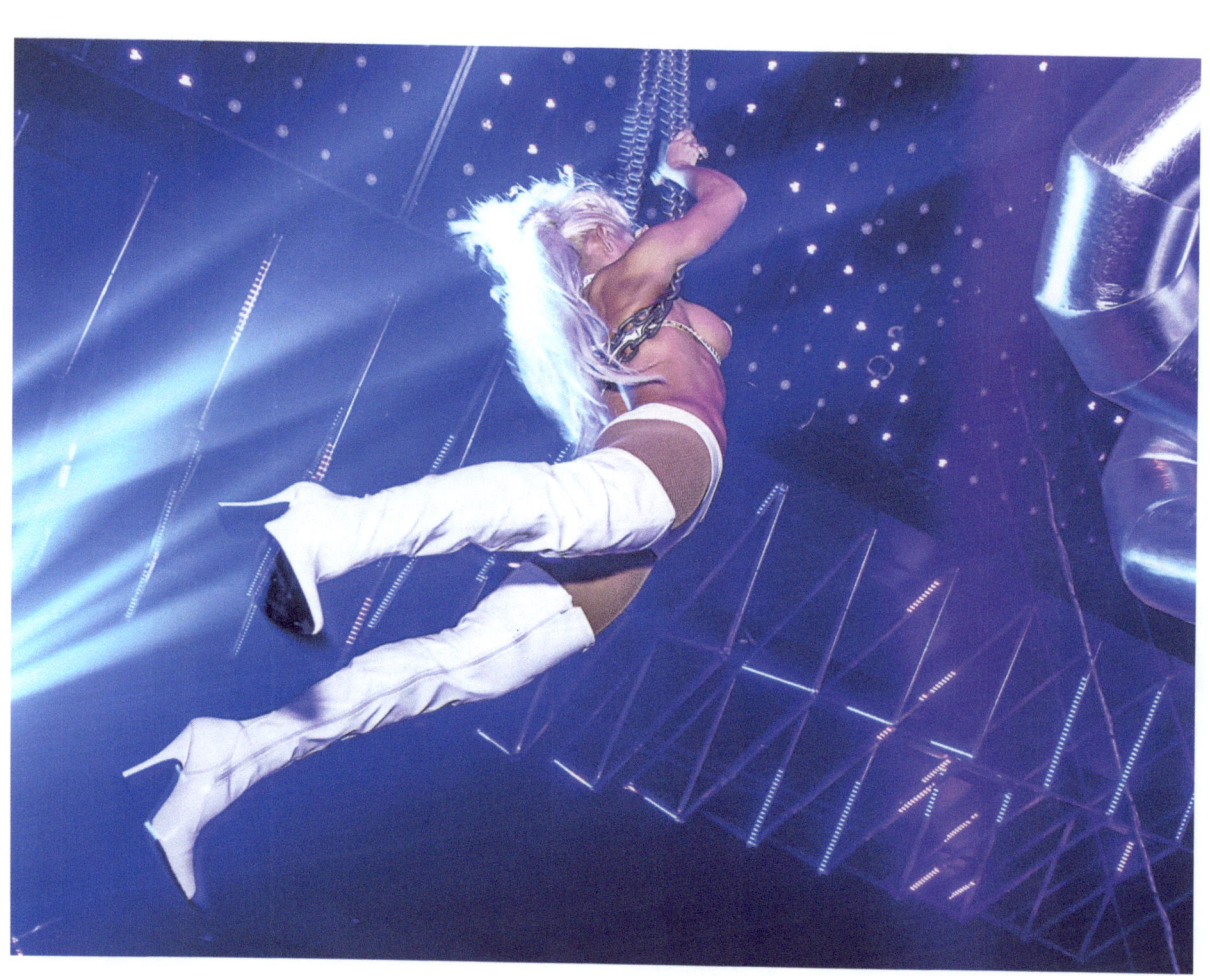

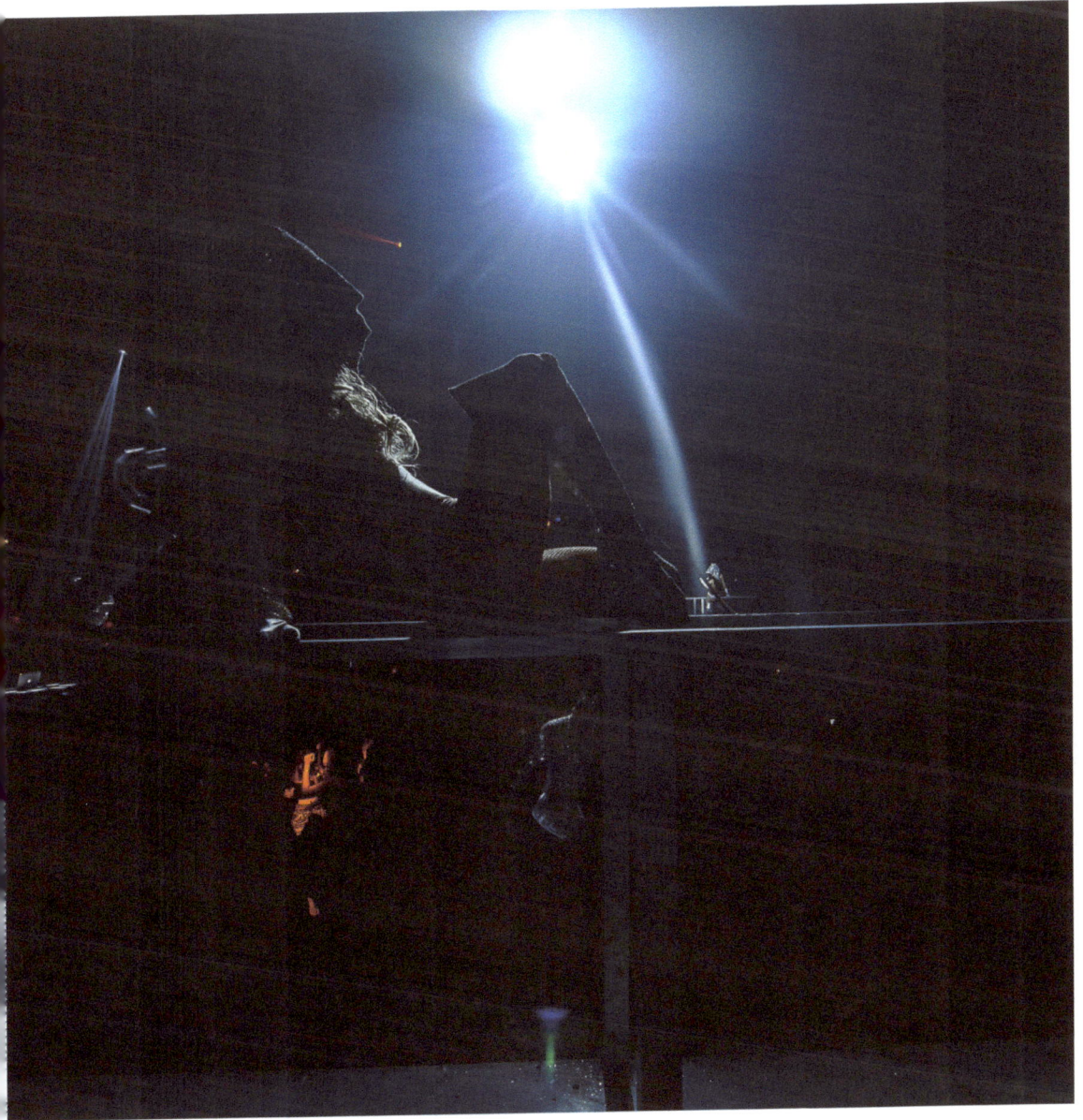

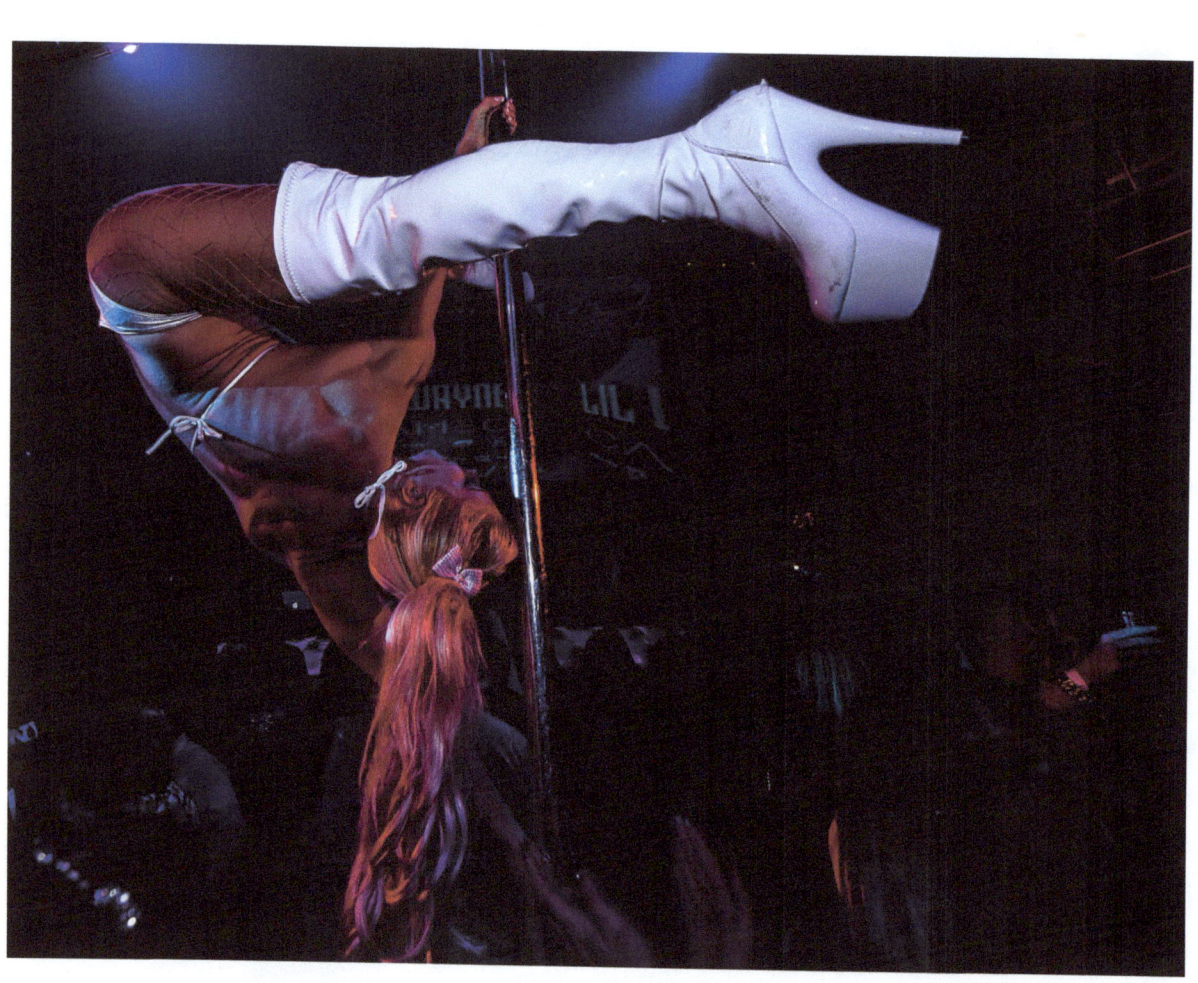

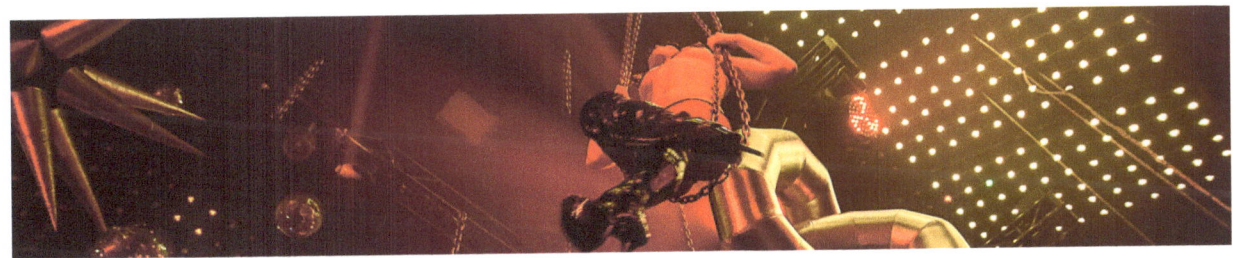

SPECIAL THANKS

In appreciation, I give special thanks to all those who supported the development of my career. In particular, special mention to my professors, family, and of course, the Night Life Performers.

Thanks.

Rodneystewartstudio@gmail.com
RodneyStewartPhotography.com